Apache Solr for Indexing Data

Enhance your Solr indexing experience with advanced techniques and the built-in functionalities available in Apache Solr

Sachin Handiekar

Anshul Johri

PUBLISHING

BIRMINGHAM - MUMBAI

Apache Solr for Indexing Data

First published: December 2015

Production reference: 1151215

Published by Packt Publishing Ltd.
Livery Place
35 Livery Street
Birmingham B3 2PB, UK.

ISBN 978-1-78355-323-5

www.packtpub.com

Credits

Authors

Sachin Handiekar

Anshul Johri

Reviewers

Damiano Braga

Florian Hopf

Commissioning Editor

Ashwin Nair

Acquisition Editors

Rebecca Pedley

Reshma Raman

Content Development Editor

Rohit Kumar Singh

Technical Editor

Utkarsha S. Kadam

Copy Editor

Vikrant Phadke

Project Coordinator

Mary Alex

Proofreader

Safis Editing

Indexer

Rekha Nair

Production Coordinator

Manu Joseph

Cover Work

Manu Joseph

About the Authors

Sachin Handiekar is a senior software developer with over 5 years of experience in Java EE development. He graduated in computer science from the University of Greenwich, London, and currently works for a global consulting company, developing enterprise applications using various open source technologies, such as Apache Camel, ServiceMix, ActiveMQ, and ZooKeeper.

He has a lot of interest in open source projects and has contributed code to Apache Camel and developed plugins for the Spring Social, which can be found on GitHub at `https://github.com/sachin-handiekar`.

He also actively writes about enterprise application development on his blog (`http://www.sachinhandiekar.com/`).

Anshul Johri has more than 10 years of technical experience in software engineering. He did his masters in computer science from the computer science department in the University of Pune. Anshul has always been a start-up mindset guy, working on fast-paced development using cutting-edge technologies and doing multiple things at a time. His core strength has always been search technology, whereby Solr plays an important role in his career. Anshul started using Solr around 9 years ago, and since then, he has never looked back. He did better and better with Solr, whether using it or contributing to the open source search community. He has used Solr extensively in all his organizations across various projects.

As mentioned earlier, Anshul has always been a start-up mindset guy. Because of that, he has worked with many start-ups in his career so far, which includes early-age and mid-size start-ups as well. To name a few, they are Ibibo.com, Asklaila.com, Bookadda.com, and so on. His last company was Amazon, where he spent around 2 years building scalable systems for Amazon Prime (a global product). Anshul recently started his own company in India with another friend from Amazon and founded `http://www.rentomo.com/`, a unique concept of a peer-to-peer sharing platform in a trusted community. He heads the technology and other core pillars of his own start-up.

Anshul did the technical review of the book *Indexing with Solr*, published by Packt Publishing.

About the Reviewers

Damiano Braga is the technical search lead at Trulia, where he leads all the backend search and browsing-related projects. He's also an open source contributor and has participated as a speaker at the Lucene Revolution 2014, where he presented Thoth, a real-time Solr monitoring and search analysis engine. He also previously reviewed the book *Apache Solr Search Patterns*, *Packt Publishing*.

Prior to Trulia, Damiano studied and worked for the University of Ferrara (Italy), where he also completed his master's degree in computer science engineering.

Florian Hopf works as a freelance software developer and consultant in Karlsruhe, Germany. He familiarized himself with Lucene-based searching while working with different content management systems on the Java platform. He is responsible for small and large search systems, on both the Internet and Intranet, for web content and application-specific data based on Lucene, Solr, and Elasticsearch. He helps organize the local Java user group as well as the Search Meetup in Karlsruhe. Florian has also written a German book on Elasticsearch. He posts blogs at `http://blog.florian-hopf.de/`.

www.PacktPub.com

Support files, eBooks, discount offers, and more

For support files and downloads related to your book, please visit www.PacktPub.com.

Did you know that Packt offers eBook versions of every book published, with PDF and ePub files available? You can upgrade to the eBook version at www.PacktPub.com and as a print book customer, you are entitled to a discount on the eBook copy. Get in touch with us at service@packtpub.com for more details.

At www.PacktPub.com, you can also read a collection of free technical articles, sign up for a range of free newsletters and receive exclusive discounts and offers on Packt books and eBooks.

https://www2.packtpub.com/books/subscription/packtlib

Do you need instant solutions to your IT questions? PacktLib is Packt's online digital book library. Here, you can search, access, and read Packt's entire library of books.

Why subscribe?
- Fully searchable across every book published by Packt
- Copy and paste, print, and bookmark content
- On demand and accessible via a web browser

Free access for Packt account holders

If you have an account with Packt at www.PacktPub.com, you can use this to access PacktLib today and view 9 entirely free books. Simply use your login credentials for immediate access.

I would like to dedicate this book to my parents, especially my late mother, Anuradha Johri, who has always been my inspiration and my friend for life. After that I would like to thank my wife, Aparna, who is always there with me in every situation no matter how tough it is; she is someone who always makes me feel complete.

Table of Contents

Preface

Welcome to *Apache Solr for Indexing Data*. Solr is an amazing enterprise tool that gives us a search engine with various possibilities to index data and gives users a better experience. This book will cover the various indexing methods that we can use to improve the indexing process by covering step-by-step examples.

The book is all about indexing in Solr, and we'll cover all the possible topics in Solr that developers can use in their use cases by following simple examples.

What this book covers

Chapter 1, Getting Started, covers the basic setup and installation needed to run Solr. It also covers the directory structure and the main configuration files used by Solr.

Chapter 2, Understanding Analyzers, Tokenizers, and Filters, shows you the basic building blocks of Solr, such as analyzers, tokenizers, and filters. These help in the indexing of data. This chapter also covers the most commonly used components in detail and how they work together.

Chapter 3, Indexing Data, helps you get a better understanding of how indexing works in Solr by building a real-life example that covers various aspects, for example, the copy field, facet, indexing time boosting, and so on.

Chapter 4, Indexing Data – The Basic Techniques and Using Index Handlers, covers various techniques by which we can index data in Solr. This chapter explains the various request handlers that are used by Solr to index CSV, JSON, and XML data type documents.

Chapter 5, Indexing Data Using Structured Datasource Using DIH, covers how we can use indexed data from a database by using the data import handler available in Solr.

Chapter 6, Indexing Data Using Apache Tika, illustrates the integration of Apache Tika with Solr for the indexing of documents.

Chapter 7, Apache Nutch, covers the integration of Apache Nutch with Solr for indexing crawl data from the Internet.

Chapter 8, Commits, Real-Time Index Optimizations, and Atomic Updates, shows us how we can use the real-time indexing features available in Solr and utilize these features to provide a real-time search experience.

Chapter 9, Advanced Topics – Multilanguage, Deduplication, and Others, covers advanced topics such as indexing multilanguage documents and removing duplicate documents from Solr.

Chapter 10, Distributed Indexing, tells us how we can utilize SolrCloud to provide a high-availability and fault-tolerant cluster.

Chapter 11, Case Study of Using Solr in E-Commerce, covers a case study by going through easy-to-use, simple examples that can be used in an e-commerce website.

What you need for this book

We are going to cover various approaches to Solr indexing. Each chapter will introduce different approaches with different software. Also, each chapter will cover the installation steps/instructions needed to run the examples for the specific scenario.

The minimal installation which we'll need to run the example code are as follows:

- JDK 1.6+ (the JAVA_HOME variable should be set up correctly on the system path)
- Apache Solr 4.10.1
- The cURL tool (Windows users can download it from `http://curl.haxx.se/download.html`)

Who this book is for

This book is for developers who want to increase their experience of indexing in Solr by learning about the various index handlers, analyzers, and methods available in Solr. Beginner level Solr development skills are expected.

Conventions

In this book, you will find a number of text styles that distinguish between different kinds of information. Here are some examples of these styles and an explanation of their meaning.

Code words in text, database table names, folder names, filenames, file extensions, pathnames, dummy URLs, user input, and Twitter handles are shown as follows: "We can include other contexts through the use of the `include` directive."

A block of code is set as follows:

```
<solr persistent="false">
<cores adminPath="/admin/cores" defaultCoreName="core1">
<core name="core1" instanceDir="core1"/>
<core name="core2" instanceDir="core2"/>
</cores>
</solr>
```

Any command-line input or output is written as follows:

```
$cd $SOLR_HOME/example/exampledocs/
$./post.shvidcard.xml
```

New terms and **important words** are shown in bold. Words that you see on the screen, for example, in menus or dialog boxes, appear in the text like this: "Click on **Install service**. You should get a service successfully installed message."

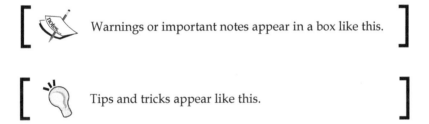

Warnings or important notes appear in a box like this.

Tips and tricks appear like this.

Reader feedback

Feedback from our readers is always welcome. Let us know what you think about this book—what you liked or disliked. Reader feedback is important for us as it helps us develop titles that you will really get the most out of.

To send us general feedback, simply e-mail `feedback@packtpub.com`, and mention the book's title in the subject of your message.

If there is a topic that you have expertise in and you are interested in either writing or contributing to a book, see our author guide at www.packtpub.com/authors.

Customer support

Now that you are the proud owner of a Packt book, we have a number of things to help you to get the most from your purchase.

Downloading the example code

You can download the example code files from your account at http://www.packtpub.com for all the Packt Publishing books you have purchased. If you purchased this book elsewhere, you can visit http://www.packtpub.com/support and register to have the files e-mailed directly to you.

Errata

Although we have taken every care to ensure the accuracy of our content, mistakes do happen. If you find a mistake in one of our books—maybe a mistake in the text or the code—we would be grateful if you could report this to us. By doing so, you can save other readers from frustration and help us improve subsequent versions of this book. If you find any errata, please report them by visiting http://www.packtpub.com/submit-errata, selecting your book, clicking on the **Errata Submission Form** link, and entering the details of your errata. Once your errata are verified, your submission will be accepted and the errata will be uploaded to our website or added to any list of existing errata under the Errata section of that title.

To view the previously submitted errata, go to https://www.packtpub.com/books/content/support and enter the name of the book in the search field. The required information will appear under the **Errata** section.

Piracy

Piracy of copyrighted material on the Internet is an ongoing problem across all media. At Packt, we take the protection of our copyright and licenses very seriously. If you come across any illegal copies of our works in any form on the Internet, please provide us with the location address or website name immediately so that we can pursue a remedy.

Please contact us at copyright@packtpub.com with a link to the suspected pirated material.

We appreciate your help in protecting our authors and our ability to bring you valuable content.

Questions

If you have a problem with any aspect of this book, you can contact us at questions@packtpub.com, and we will do our best to address the problem.

1
Getting Started

We will start this chapter with a quick overview of Solr, followed by a section that helps you get Solr up and running. We will also cover some basic building blocks of the Solr architecture, its directory structure, and its configurations files. This chapter covers following topics:

- Overview and installation of Solr
- Running Solr
- The Solr architecture and directory structure
- Multicore Solr

Overview and installation of Solr

Solr is the one of the most popular open source enterprise search platforms from the Apache Lucene open source project. Its features include full text search, faceted search, highlighting, near-real-time indexing, dynamic clustering, rich document handling, and geospatial search. Solr is highly reliable and scalable. This is the reason Solr powers the search features of the world's largest Internet sites, for example, Netflix, TicketMaster, SourceForge, and so on (source: `https://wiki.apache.org/solr/PublicServers`).

Solr is written in Java and runs as a standalone full text search server with a REST-like API. You feed documents into it (which is called indexing) via XML, JSON, CSV, and binary over HTTP. You query it through HTTP GET and receive XML, JSON, CSV, and binary results.

Let's go through the installation process of Solr. This section describes how to install Solr on various operating systems such as Mac, Windows, and Linux. Let's go through each of them one by one.

Installing Solr in OS X (Mac)

The easiest way to install Solr on OS X is by using **homebrew**. If you are not aware of homebrew and don't have homebrew installed on your Mac, then go to http://brew.sh/. Homebrew is the easiest way of installing packages/software on Mac.

You will require JRE 1.7 or above to install Solr on OS X. Just type java -version in the terminal and see what the version of JRE installed in your computer is. If it's less than 1.7, then you need to upgrade it to higher version and proceed with the following instructions.

Just type the following command in the terminal and it will automatically download all the files needed for Solr. Sit back and relax for a few minutes until it completes:

```
$ brew install Solr
```

Running Solr

To test whether your installation was completed successfully, you need to run Solr. Type these commands in the terminal to run it:

```
$ cd /usr/local/Cellar/solr/4.4.0/libexec/example/
$ java -jar start.jar
```

After you run the preceding commands, you will see lots of dumping messages/logs on the terminal. Don't worry! It's normal. Just try to fix any error if it is there. Once the messages are stopped and there is no error message, simply go to any web browser and type http://localhost:8983/solr/#/.

Downloading the example code

You can download the example code files from your account at http://www.packtpub.com for all the Packt Publishing books you have purchased. If you purchased this book elsewhere, you can visit http://www.packtpub.com/support and register to have the files e-mailed directly to you.

You will see following screen on your browser:

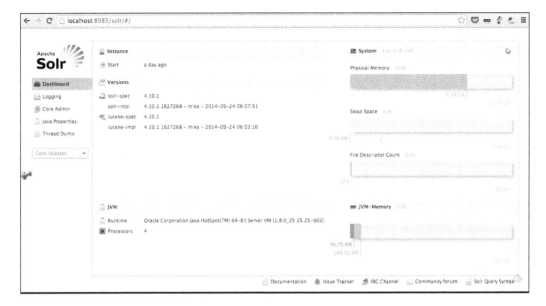

Fresh Solr do not contain any data. In Solr terminology, data is termed as a document. You will learn how to index data in Solr in upcoming chapters.

Installing Solr in Windows

There are multiple ways of installing Solr on a Windows machine. Here, I have explained the way to set up Solr with Jetty running as a service via NSSM:

1. Install the latest Java JDK from `http://www.oracle.com/technetwork/java/javase/downloads/index.html`.

2. Download the latest Solr release (ZIP version) from `http://www.apache.org/dyn/closer.cgi/lucene/solr/`. At the time of writing this book, the latest Solr release was 4.10.1.

3. Unzip the Solr download. You should have files as shown in the following screenshot. Open the example folder.

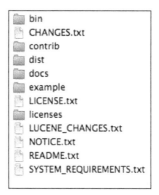

4. Copy the etc, lib, logs, solr, and webapps folders and start.jar to C:\solr (you will need to create the folder at C:\solr), as shown in the following screenshot:

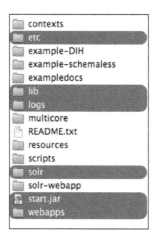

5. Now open the C:\solr\solr folder and copy the contents back to the root C:\solr folder. When you are done, you can delete the C:\solr\solr folder. See the following image, the selected folder you can delete now:

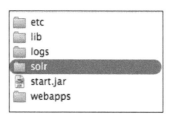

At this point, your C:\solr directory should look like what is shown in the following screenshot:

6. Solr can be run at this point if you start it from the command line. Change your directory to C:\solr and then run java -Dsolr.solr. home=C:/solr/ -jar start.jar.

7. If you go to http://localhost:8983/solr/, you should see the Solr dashboard.

8. Now Solr is up and running, so we can work on getting Jetty to run as a Windows service. Since Jetty comes bundled with Solr, all that we need to do is run it as a service. There are several options to do this, but the one I prefer is through **Non-Sucking Service Manager (NSSM)**program in windows which is the, the most compatible service manager across Windows environment. NSSM can be downloaded from http://nssm.cc/download.

9. Once you have downloaded NSSM, open the win32 or win64 folder as appropriate and copy nssm.exe to your C:\solr folder.

10. Open Command Prompt, change the directory to C:\solr, and then run nssm install Solr.

11. A dialog will open. Select java.exe as the application located at C:\Windows\System32\.

12. In the options input box, enter: Dsolr.solr.home=C:/solr/ -Djetty. home=C:/solr/ -Djetty.logs=C:/solr/logs/ -cp C:/solr/lib/*. jar;C:/solr/start.jar -jar C:/solr/start.jar.

13. Click on **Install service**. You should get a service successfully installed message.

14. Finally run net start Solr.

15. Jetty should now be running as a service. Check this by going to http://localhost:/8983/solr/.

Installing Solr on Linux

To install Solr on Linux/Unix, you will need **Java Runtime Environment (JRE)** version 1.7 or higher. Then follow these steps:

1. Download the latest Solr release (`.tgz`) from `http://www.apache.org/dyn/closer.cgi/lucene/solr/`. At the time of writing this book, the latest release was 4.10.1.

2. Unpack the file to your desired location.

3. Solr runs inside a Java servlet container, such as Tomcat, Jetty, and so on. Solr distribution includes a working demo server in the `example` directory, which runs in Jetty. You can use Jetty servlet container, or use your preferred servlet container. If you are using a servlet container other than Jetty and it's already running, then stop that server.

4. Copy the `solr-4.10.1.war` file from the Solr distribution under the `dist` directory to the `webapps` directory of your servlet container. Change the name of this file; it must be named `solr.war`.

5. Copy the Solr home directory, `solr-4.x.0/example/solr/`, from the distribution to your desired Solr home location.

6. Start your servlet container, passing to it the location of your Solr home in one of these ways:

    1. Set the `solr.solr.home` Java system property to your `Solr home` (for example, using this example jetty setup: `java -Dsolr.solr.home=/some/dir -jar start.jar`).

    2. Configure the `servlet` container so that a JNDI lookup of `java:comp/env/solr/home` by the Solr web app will point to your `Solr Home`.

    3. Start the `servlet` container in the directory containing `./solr`. The default `Solr Home` is `solr` under the JVM's current working directory (`$CWD/solr`).

7. To confirm the installation, just go to `http://localhost:/8983/solr/` and you will see the Solr dashboard. Now your Solr is up and running.

Thus, by the end of the installation, your Solr is up and running. But since we have not fed any data into Solr, it will not index any data. Let's try to insert some example data into our server.

The Solr download comes with example data bundled in it. We can use the same data for indexing as an example. Go to the `exampledocs` directory under the example directory. Here, you will see a lot of files. Now go to the command line (terminal) and type the following commands:

```
$ cd $SOLR_HOME/example/exampledocs/
$ ./post.sh vidcard.xml
```

Within the `post.sh` file, the script will call `http://localhost:8983/solr/update` using `curl` to post `xml` data from the `vidcard.xml` file. When the import completes (without any error), you will see a message that looks something like this:

```
Posting file vidcard.xml to http://localhost:8983/solr/update
<?xml version="1.0" encoding="UTF-8"?>
<response>
<lst name="responseHeader"><int name="status">0</int><int name="QTime">562</int></lst>
</response>

<?xml version="1.0" encoding="UTF-8"?>
<response>
<lst name="responseHeader"><int name="status">0</int><int name="QTime">165</int></lst>
</response>
```

Now let's try to check out our imported data from web browser. Try `http://localhost:8983/solr/select?q=*:*&wt=json` to fetch all of the data in your Solr instance, like this:

When you see the preceding data, it means that your Solr server is running properly and is ready to index your desired feed. You will be reading indexing in depth in upcoming chapters.

The Solr architecture and directory structure

In real-world scenarios, Solr runs with other applications on a web server. A typical example is an online store application. The store provides a user interface, a shopping cart, an items catalogue, and a way to make purchases. It needs to store this information some sort of database. Here, Solr makes easy so add the capability of searching data in the online store. To make data searchable, you need to feed it to Solr for indexing. Data can be fed to Solr in various ways and also in various formats, such as .pdf, .doc, .txt, and so on. In the process of feeding data to Solr, you need to define a schema. A schema is a way of telling Solr about data and how you want to make your data indexed. A lot many factors need to be considered while feeding data, which we will discuss in detail in upcoming chapters.

Solr queries are RESTful, which means that a Solr query is just a simple HTTP request and the response is a structured document, mainly in XML, but it could be JSON, CSV, or any other format as well based on your requirement. A typical architecture of Solr in the real world looks something like this:

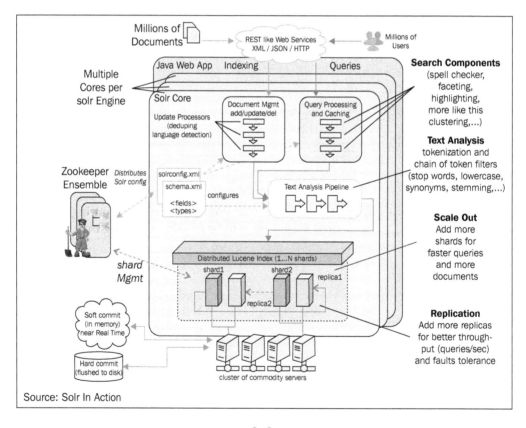

Do not worry if you are not able to understand the preceding diagram right now. We will cover every component related to indexing in detail. The purpose of this diagram is to give you a feel of the current architecture of Solr and its working in the real world. If you see the preceding diagram properly, you will find two `.xml` files named `schema.xml` and `solrconfig.xml`. These are the two most important files in the Solr configuration and are considered the building blocks of Solr.

Solr directory structure

Here's the directory layout of a typical `Solr Home` directory:

```
|  + conf
|      - schema.xml
|      - solrconfig.xml
|      - stopwords.txt
|      - synonyms.txt etc
|  + data
|      - index
|      - spellchecker
```

Let's get a brief understanding of `solrconfig.xml` and `schema.xml` here before we proceed further, as these are the building blocks of Solr (as stated earlier). We will cover them in detail in the next few chapters.

The `solrconfig.xml` file is the core configuration file of Solr, with most parameters affecting Solr itself directly. This file can be found in the `solr/collection1/conf/` directory. When configuring Solr, you'll work with `solrconfig.xml` often. The file consists of a series of XML statements that set configuration values, and some of the most important configurations are:

* Defining `data dir` (the directory where indexed files remain)
* Request handlers (handle upcoming HTTP requests)
* Listeners
* Request dispatchers (used to manage HTTP communications)
* Admin web interface settings
* Replication and duplication parameters

These are some of the important configurations defined in `solrconfig.xml`. This file is well commented; I would advise you to go through it from the start and read all the comments. You will get a very good understanding of the various components involved in the Solr configuration.

The second most important configuration file is called `schema.xml`. This file can be found in the `solr/collection1/conf/` directory. As the name says, this file is used to define the schema of the data (content) that you want to index and make searchable. Data is called **document** in Solr terminology. The `schema.xml` file contains all the details about the fields that your documents can contain, and how these fields should be dealt with when adding documents to the index or when querying those fields. This file can be divided broadly into two sections:

- The types section (the definitions of all types)
- The fields section (the definitions of the document structure using types)

The structure of your document should be defined as a field under the `fields` section. Let's say you have to define a book as a document in Solr with fields as `isbn`, `title`, `author`, and `price`. The schema will be as follows:

```
<field name="isbn" type="string" required="true" indexed="true"
stored="true"/> <field name="title" type="text_general"
indexed="true" stored="true"/>
<field name="author" type="text-general" indexed="true"
stored="true" multiValued="true"/>
<field name="price" type="int" indexed="true" stored="true"/>
```

In the preceding schema, you see a `type` attribute, which defines the data type of the field. You can change the behavior of the field by changing the type. The `multiValued` attribute is used to tell Solr that the field can hold multiple values, while the `required` attribute makes the field mandatory for creating a document. After the `fields` section ends, we need to mention which field is going to be unique. In our case, it is going to be `isbn`:

```
<uniqueKey>isbn</uniqueKey>
```

The `schema.xml` file is also well-commented file. I will again advise you to go through the comments of this file, for starting this will help you understand the various field types and data types in detail.

Cores in Solr (Multicore Solr)

Solr cores make it possible to run multiple indexes with different configurations and schemas in a single Solr instance. The multicore feature of Solr helps in unified administration of Solr instances for complete and different applications. Cores in Solr are fairly isolated and have their own configuration and schema files. This helps manage cores at runtime (create or remove) from a Solr instance without restarting the process.

Cores in Solr are managed through a configuration file called `solr.xml`. The `solr.xml` file is present in your `Solr Home` directory. Since its inception, `solr.xml` has evolved from configuring one core to managing multiple cores and eventually defining parameters for `SolrCloud`. Do not worry much about `SolrCloud` if you are not aware of it, as we have a dedicated chapter that covers `SolrCloud` in detail. In brief, `SolrCloud` is a terminology used in distributed search and indexing. When we need to index huge amounts of data, we need to think of scalability and performance. This is where `SolrCloud` comes into the picture.

Starting from Solr 4.3, Solr will maintain two distinct formats for `solr.xml`; one is legacy and the other is discovery mode. The legacy format will be supported until the 4.x.0 series and it will be deprecated in the 5.0 release of Solr. The default `solr.xml` config file looks something like this:

```
<solr>

  <solrcloud>
    <str name="host">${host:}</str>
    <int name="hostPort">${jetty.port:8983}</int>
    <str name="hostContext">${hostContext:solr}</str>
    <int name="zkClientTimeout">${zkClientTimeout:30000}</int>
    <bool
      name="genericCoreNodeNames">${genericCoreNodeNames:true}</bool>
  </solrcloud>

  <shardHandlerFactory name="shardHandlerFactory"
    class="HttpShardHandlerFactory">
    <int name="socketTimeout">${socketTimeout:0}</int>
    <int name="connTimeout">${connTimeout:0}</int>
  </shardHandlerFactory>

</solr>
```

The preceding configuration shows that Solr configurations are `SolrCloud` friendly, but this does not mean that Solr is running in SolrCloud mode, unless you start Solr with some special parameters (explained in the SolrCloud *Chapter 10, Distributed Indexing*). To configure multiple cores in Solr in legacy format, you need to edit the `solr.xml` file with the following code snippet and remove the existing discovery code from `solr.xml`:

```
<solr persistent="false">
    <cores adminPath="/admin/cores" defaultCoreName="core1">
    <core name="core1" instanceDir="core1" />
    <core name="core2" instanceDir="core2" />
  </cores>
</solr>
```

Now you need to create two cores (new directories, `core1` and `core2`) in the `Solr` directory. You also need to create Solr configuration files for new cores. To do this, just copy the same configuration files (the `conf` directory in `collections1`) in both cores for now and restart the Solr server after you have made these settings.

Once you restart the Solr server with the preceding configuration, two cores will be created, with names `core1` and `core2` and the existing default Solr configuration settings. The `instanceDir` variable defines the directory name relative to `solr.xml` — where to look for configuration and data files. You can modify the paths of these cores according to your wishes and the configuration files according to your use case. You can also change the names of the cores.

You can verify your settings by opening the following URL in your browser: `http://localhost:8983/solr/`.

You will see two new cores created in the Solr dashboard. Currently, there is no document in any of the cores because we have not indexed any data so far. So, this concludes the process of creating multiple cores in Solr.

Summary

Thus, by the end of the first chapter, you have learned what Solr is, how to install and run it on various operating systems, what the various components and basic building blocks of Solr are (such as its configuration files and directory structure), and how to set up configuration files. You also learned in brief about the architecture of Solr. In the last section, we covered multicore setup in the Solr 4.x.0 series. However, the legacy method of multicore setup is going to be deprecated in the Solr 5.x release and then it's going to be only discovery mode, which is called **SolrCloud**.

In the next chapter, we will look deeply into the various components used in Solr configuration files, such as tokenizers, analyzers, filters, field types, and so on.

2
Understanding Analyzers, Tokenizers, and Filters

In the previous chapter, we read how to install and run Solr on various operating systems and covered its architecture. We talked briefly about the basic building blocks of Solr, such as Solr config files.

In this chapter, we will cover the following core components of the Solr configuration:

- Analyzers
- Tokenizers
- Filters

Introducing analyzers

To make us able to search effectively and efficiently, Solr splits text into tokens during indexing as well as during search (query time). Solr does all of this with the help of its three main components: analyzers, tokenizers, and filters. Analyzers are used during both indexing and searching. An analyzer examines the text of fields and the generated token stream with the help of tokenizers. Then, filters examine the stream of tokens and perform filtering jobs of any one of these: keeping them, discarding them, or creating new tokens. Tokenizers and filters might be combined in the form of pipelines or chains such that the output of one is the input of the other. Such a sequence of tokenizers and filters is called an analyzer, and the resulting output of the analyzer is used to match search queries or build indices. Let's see how we can use these components in Solr and implement them.

Analyzers are core components that preprocess input text at indexing and search time. It's recommended that you use similar or the same analyzers to preprocess text in a compatible manner at query and index time. In simple terms, the role of an analyzer is to examine the input text and generate token streams. An analyzer is specified as a child of a `<fieldType>` element in the `schema.xml` configuration file.

In normal usage, only fields of the `solr.TextField` type specify an analyzer. There are two ways to specify how text fields are analyzed in Solr with the help of analyzers in `schema.xml`:

- One way is to specify the class name of an analyzer whose class attribute is a fully qualified Java class name. This is the simplest way of configuring an analyzer with a single `<analyzer>` element. The class name must be derived from `org.apache.lucene.analysis.Analyzer`. The following is an example:

```
<fieldType name="nametext" class="solr.TextField">
  <analyzer
class="org.apache.lucene.analysis.WhitespaceAnalyzer"/>
</fieldType>
```

  In this case, a single class, `WhitespaceAnalyzer`, is responsible for analyzing the content of the named text field and emitting the corresponding tokens. This analyzer can be used in simple cases where only plain English input text is present. But in general, there is always more complex analysis that is done on field content.

- The second way is to specify a `TokenizerFactory` followed by a list of optional `TokenFilterFactory`, which are applied in the listed order. This is the way of performing complex analyses on input text content; for example, you can decompose your analysis into discrete and relatively simple steps. Here is an example:

```
<fieldType name="nametext" class="solr.TextField">
  <analyzer>
    <tokenizer class="solr.StandardTokenizerFactory"/>
    <filter class="solr.StandardFilterFactory"/>
    <filter class="solr.LowerCaseFilterFactory"/>
    <filter class="solr.StopFilterFactory"/>
    <filter class="solr.EnglishPorterFilterFactory"/>
  </analyzer>
</fieldType>
```

In the preceding case, we are trying to set up an analysis chain by simply specifying the `<analyzer>` element (no class attribute) and child elements, which are factory classes for the tokenizers and filters in the order that you want to run. In this case, no analyzer class is defined in the `<analyzer>` element. Rather, there is a sequence of more specialized classes clubbed together to act as an analyzer for the field which is going to be analyzed. Soon, you will discover that a Solr distribution comes with a large selection of tokenizers and filters that will help by covering most of the scenarios that you are likely to encounter.

 Note that classes in the `org.apache.solr.analysis` package may be referred to here with the short alias `solr.prefix`.

We will cover tokenizers and filters in detail in upcoming topics.

Analysis phases

We read earlier that analysis happens in two contexts. At index time, when a field is being created, the token stream that results from the analysis is added to the index and defines a set of terms such as position, size, and so on for the field. At query time, the search query is analyzed and the terms are matched against those that are stored in the field's index. In many cases, the same analysis is used at index and query time, but there might be some cases in which you may want to use different steps of analysis during indexing and search time. Here is an example of this:

```
<fieldType name="nametext" class="solr.TextField">
  <analyzer type="index">
    <tokenizer class="solr.StandardTokenizerFactory"/>
    <filter class="solr.LowerCaseFilterFactory"/>
    filter class="solr.RemoveWordFilterFactory"
      words="removewords.txt"/>
    <filter class="solr.SynonymFilterFactory"
      synonyms="synonyms.txt"/>
  </analyzer>
  <analyzer type="query">
    <tokenizer class="solr.StandardTokenizerFactory"/>
    <filter class="solr.LowerCaseFilterFactory"/>
  </analyzer>
</fieldType>
```

In the preceding example, you can see that we have used two `<analyzer>` definitions, distinguished by the `type` attribute. Based on the `type` attribute, Solr applies the analyzer to the input field at `index` and `query` time. At the time of indexing data, we told the analyzer to follow different steps, in comparison to query time. At index time, we told Solr to tokenize the text using the `solr.StandardTokenizerFactory` class, after which we used a filter called `solr.LowerCaseFilterFactory` to make the tokens lowercase. After making the tokens lowercase, we used another filter called `solr.RemoveWordFilterFactory`, which removes the tokens as per the words defined in `removewords.txt`. The final filter that we used maps the tokens to an alternate value using the `solr.SynonymFilterFactory` filter, which uses the `synonyms.txt` file. But at `query` time, we asked analyzer to apply only the lowercase filter to convert query terms to lowercase. Other filters that were applied at `index` time were not applied at `query` time.

Tokenizers

The function of a tokenizer is to break input text into tokens, where each token is a stream of characters in the text. You configure a tokenizer for a text field type in `schema.xml` with a `<tokenizer>` element, which is a child of `<analyzer>`, like this for example:

```
<fieldType name="text" class="solr.TextField">
    <analyzer type="index">
        <tokenizer class="solr.StandardTokenizerFactory"/>
        <filter class="solr.StandardFilterFactory"/>
    </analyzer>
</fieldType>
```

In the preceding example, you can see that a class attribute names a factory class that will instantiate a tokenizer object when needed. Tokenizer factory classes implement `org.apache.solr.analysis.TokenizerFactory`. You can pass arguments to tokenizer factories by setting attributes in the `<tokenizer>` element. Here is an example of this:

```
<fieldType name="semicolonDelimited" class="solr.TextField">
  <analyzer type="query">
  <tokenizer class="solr.PatternTokenizerFactory" pattern="; "/>
  <analyzer>
</fieldType>
```

In the preceding example, the `PatternTokenizerFactory` class implements `org.apache.solr.analysis.TokenizerFactory` and an argument is passed to this class with the attribute name pattern.

There are a lot of factory classes that are included in the Solr release. Let's go through some of them.

Standard tokenizer

The standard tokenizer splits input text into tokens considering whitespaces and punctuations as delimiters. This is the most used tokenizer in Solr configuration. Here is an example of it:

```
<analyzer>
  <tokenizer class="solr.StandardTokenizerFactory"/>
</analyzer>
```

Input text: `"Hello, packt.pub@uk.com 01-17, re: m56-nm."`

Output: `"Hello"`, `"packt.pub"`, `"uk.com"`, `"01"`, `"17"`, `"re"`, `"m56"`, `"xq"`

In this tokenizer, delimiter characters are discarded, with the following exceptions:

- Periods (dots) that are not followed by whitespaces are kept as part of the token, including Internet domain names
- The @ character belongs to the set of token-splitting punctuation, so e-mail addresses are not preserved as single tokens

Keyword tokenizer

The keyword tokenizer treats the entire input text as a single token. An example of it is as follows:

```
<analyzer>
  <tokenizer class="solr.KeywordTokenizerFactory"/>
</analyzer>
```

Input text: `"Hello, packt.pub@uk.com 01-17, re: m56-nm."`

Output: `"Hello, packt.pub@uk.com 01-17, re: m56-nm."`

Lowercase tokenizer

As the name suggests, the lowercase tokenizer tokenizes the input text by delimiting at non-letters and converting all letters to lowercase. In this tokenizer, whitespaces and non-letters are discarded. Here is an example of it:

```
<analyzer>
  <tokenizer class="solr.LowerCaseTokenizerFactory"/>
</analyzer>
```

Input text: `"I LOVE Packtpub Books!"`

Output: `"i"`, `"love"`, `"packtpub"`, `"books"`

N-gram tokenizer

The N-gram tokenizer reads the input text and generates N-gram tokens based on the input parameters of sizes in the given range. An example of this tokenizer is as follows:

```
<analyzer>
  <tokenizer class="solr.NGramTokenizerFactory"/>
</analyzer>
```

The default behavior of this tokenizer is not to break the field at whitespaces. So, the resulting output in this example contains a whitespace as a token. The default minimum gram size is 1 and the maximum gram size is 2.

Input text: `"packt pub"`

Output: `"p"`, `"a"`, `"c"`, `"k"`, `"t"`, `" "`, `"p"`, `"u"`, `"b"`, `"pa"`, `"ck"`, `"t "`, `" p"`, `"ub"`

The following is an example with an N-gram size of 4 to 5:

```
<analyzer>
  <tokenizer class="solr.NGramTokenizerFactory" minGramSize="4"
    maxGramSize="5"/>
</analyzer>
```

Input text: `"packtpub"`

Output: `"pack"`, `"packt"`, `"ackt"`, `"acktp"`, `"cktp"`, `"cktpu"`, `"ktpu"`, `"ktpub"`, `"tpub"`

Other widely used tokenizers are:

- Letter tokenizer
- Classic tokenizer
- Whitespace tokenizer
- Edge N-gram tokenizer
- ICU tokenizer
- Path hierarchy tokenizer
- Regular-expression tokenizer
- UAX29 URL e-mail tokenizer

You can go through the `schema.xml` file, and you will see good examples of tokenizers and their use cases. This file has well-commented sections.

Filters

Like tokenizers, filters consume tokens as input and again produce a stream of tokens. The function of a filter is a bit different from that of a tokenizer. Unlike a tokenizer, a filter receives tokens as the input (passed by a tokenizer), and its function is to look at each token and decide whether to keep this token, change/replace it, or discard it. Filters are also derive from `org.apache.lucene.analysis.TokenStream`.

A typical example of a filter looks something like this:

```
<fieldType name="text" class="solr.TextField">
  <analyzer>
    <tokenizer class="solr.StandardTokenizerFactory"/>
    <filter class="solr.StandardFilterFactory"/>
    <filter class="solr.LowerCaseFilterFactory"/>
  </analyzer>
</fieldType>
```

Filters are configured in `schema.xml` with a `<filter>` element as a child of `<analyzer>`, following the `<tokenizer>` element. Since filters take token streams as input, the filter definition should follow the tokenizer or another filter definition, as shown in the preceding example.

The preceding example starts with a standard tokenizer; it tokenizes the input text. Then these tokens pass through Solr's standard filter, which removes dots from acronyms and performs some other common operations. All the tokens are then set to lowercase, which will help in case-insensitive matching at query time.

Like tokenizers, the class attribute names a factory class that instantiates a filter object as needed. Filter factory classes must implement the `org.apache.solr.analysis.TokenFilterFactory` interface. Arguments may be passed to tokenizer factories to change their behavior by setting attributes in the `<filter>` element. An example of filter factory is as follows:

```
<fieldType name="hyphenDelimited" class="solr.TextField">
  <analyzer type="query">
    <tokenizer class="solr.PatternTokenizerFactory" pattern="- "
      />
    <filter class="solr.LengthFilterFactory" min="3" max="6"/>
  </analyzer>
</fieldType>
```

Let's see some of the filter factories that are included in the Solr release.

Lowercase filter

The lowercase filter converts all uppercase letters to lowercase tokens, and all other characters are left unchanged:

```
<analyzer>
  <tokenizer class="solr.StandardTokenizerFactory"/>
  <filter class="solr.LowerCaseFilterFactory"/>
</analyzer>
```

Input text: `"I Love Apache Solr"`

Tokenizer input to filter: `"I", "Love", "Apache", "Solr"`

Output: `"i", "love", "apache", "solr"`

Synonym filter

The synonym filter is responsible for synonym mapping. Each token is matched with a list of synonyms present in the synonym file passed as an argument, and if a match is found, then the synonym is put in place of the token:

```
<analyzer>
  <tokenizer class="solr.StandardTokenizerFactory"/>
  <filter class="solr.SynonymFilterFactory"
    synonyms="synonyms.txt"/>
</analyzer>
```

The format of the `synonyms.txt` file is as follows:

```
i-phone, i phone, iphone  => iphone
iit, IIT, I.I.T => Indian Institute of Technology
small => tiny, short, teeny
```

Input text: "new i-phone is small"

Tokenizer input to filter: "new", "i-phone", "is", "small"

Output: "new", "iphone", "is", "tiny", "short", "teeny"

Porter stem filter

The **Porter** stem filter applies the Porter stemming algorithm for the English language. This filter is very similar to the Snowball Porter stem filter with the English language. In the snowball porter stem filter, you can provide a language as the input parameter, such as French, Spanish, and so on:

```
<analyzer type="index">
  <tokenizer class="solr.StandardTokenizerFactory "/>
  <filter class="solr.PorterStemFilterFactory"/>
</analyzer>
```

Input text: "run runs running ran"

Tokenizer input to filter: "run", "runs", "running", "ran"

Output: "run", "run", "run", "run"

Other filters are:

- Length filter
- Keep words filter
- ICU transform filter
- KStem filter
- N-gram filter
- Pattern replace filter
- Position filter factory
- Remove duplicates token filter
- Shingle filter
- Reversed wildcard filter

- Token offset payload filter
- Trim filter
- Type token filter
- Word delimiter filter

Running your analyzer

Once you are done with configuring your Solr according to your use case, such as analyzers, tokenizers, and filters, you can actually test your configuration without indexing data. The Solr admin interface provides a very clean and easy way to test your configuration. Refer to the following screenshot to see analyzer page for core1:

Let's create a new field type and put the following configuration into `schema.xml`:

```xml
<fieldType name="mytextfield" class="solr.TextField">
  <analyzer type="index">
    <tokenizer class="solr.WhitespaceTokenizerFactory"/>
    <filter class="solr.HyphenatedWordsFilterFactory"/>
    <filter class="solr.LowerCaseFilterFactory"/>
  </analyzer>
  <analyzer type="query">
    <tokenizer class="solr.StandardTokenizerFactory"/>
    <filter class="solr.LowerCaseFilterFactory"/>
  </analyzer>
</fieldType>
```

Now restart your Solr and go to the analyzer. Next, choose your defined field type, **mytextfield**, from the dropdown, like this:

Now you can type your input text and see how Solr indexes your data. You can play with different pieces of input text and analyze your analyzer setting for each field. Based on your use case, you can further modify your field type. Here is an example of this:

Summary

In this chapter, we saw how we can use analyzers, tokenizers, and filters in Solr, which gives us the ability to transform data during index and query time. We also saw how we can remove words using the `solr.RemoveWordFilterFactory` filter and use `solr.StandardTokenizerFactory` to tokenize text that is getting indexed into Solr.

In the next chapter, we'll see how we can use the components that we've discussed in this chapter to create a schema.

3
Indexing Data

In the previous chapter, we saw the various analyzers, tokenizers, and filters provided by Solr that help us select the most important data from a given document. In this chapter, we'll see how Solr provides us a way to index this data so that we can run queries on top of it. We'll cover the following topics in this chapter:

- Defining field types in Solr
- Creating a custom `musicCatalogue` example
- Facet searching

The Solr indexing process can mainly be broken down into two major parts:

- Converting the document from its native format to XML or JSON, both of which are supported by Solr
- Adding documents into Solr datastore using API or HTTP POST

To better understand the preceding two parts, we'll create an example of a music catalogue that contains metadata related to songs. The music catalogue will contain metadata related to a song that can later be used to retrieve important information regarding the song.

We'll also see how Solr provides various ways of feeding this information into it and how we can retrieve it.

Indexing data in Solr

Indexing of data in Solr is done using a document that contains fields that are used to provide major information to Solr. A document can be broken down further into fields, which contain major pieces of information that is used by Solr to further provide better search results.

The `musicCatalogue` core that we'll build will contain fields representing information related to a song. For example, an `artistName` field will contain the name of the artist who sang the song. Another field such as `duration` can contain the length of the song. A fields can also contain a data type, which will further describe the type of data that can be used. For example, `artistName` can be described as a text field. On the other hand, the `duration` field can be of type float or double. The `fieldType` property specifies the kind of field to be used by Solr.

> More information about floating-point numbers can be found at https://en.wikipedia.org/wiki/Floating_point.

So let's go ahead and create a schema for our `musicCatalogue` example. As we progress through this chapter, we'll see what Solr provides us when we create a schema for our `musicCatalogue` example.

To create our example, we'll use the default installation of Solr that we set up in *Chapter 1, Getting Started*. We will do so to create a core for our `musicCatalogue`.

We'll create a directory called `musicCatalog` in `SOLR_HOME//solr`. After we have created a directory, we'll create a folder named `conf` to hold `schema.xml` and `solrconfig.xml`, which will be used by Solr:

```
music-catalog
\---conf
        schema.xml
        solrconfig.xml
```

The `schema.xml` config will define the fields that are necessary for our `musicCatalogue` example. To keep the music catalogue simple, we're going to use the following fields only:

Field name	Data type	Solr field type
songId	Long	solr.TrieLongField
songName	String	solr.StrField
artistName	String	solr.StrField
albumArtist	String	solr.StrField
songDuration	Double	solr.TrieDoubleField
Rating	Float	solr.TrieFloatField
Composer	String	solr.StrField

Field name	Data type	Solr field type
Rating	Float	solr.TrieFloatField
Year	Integer	solr.intField
Genre	String	solr.StrField

So let's see what our `schema.xml` file should look like and the various fields and field types that we can use while building this schema.

A basic `schema.xml` file looks like this:

```
<?xml version="1.0" encoding="UTF-8" ?>
<schema name="uniqueSchemaName" version="1.5">
<!--More elements go here -->
</schema>
```

As we can see from the preceding XML, every schema must consist of a unique name that will distinguish it from others.

For this example, we'll name it `musicCatalogue`. A schema can contain the following elements within it:

- Field types
- Fields, copyFields, and dynamicFields
- A unique key
- A Solr query parser
- A copy field
- Similarity

Introducing field types

A field type in Solr defines how data should be interpreted and how Solr can use it to index the data. A field type can contain an analyzer and a filter, which we've seen in *Chapter 2, Understanding Analyzers, Tokenizers, and Filters*. These help Solr refine the data that it needs to index.

To keep it simple, we won't be using any filters or analyzers in our example. For our example, we've defined the following field types:

```
<fieldType name="int" class="solr.TrieIntField"/>
<fieldType name="float" class="solr.TrieFloatField"/>
<fieldType name="string" class="solr.StrField"/>
<fieldType name="double" class="solr.TrieDoubleField"/>
<fieldType name="long" class="solr.TrieLongField"/>
```

As we can see from the `fieldType` element contains the following main attributes:

- `name`: This attribute contains the name of the `fieldType` elements, which can be used later on while defining the field element
- `class`: This is the Solr class that can be used to denote the data type used

By default Solr supports various data types that we can use when creating a schema.

 A list of these field types can be found in the Solr documentation at `https://cwiki.apache.org/confluence/display/solr/Field+Types+Included+with+Solr`.

After creating the field type element within our schema, let's create the major fields that are necessary for storing information related to the music catalogue.

Defining fields

Fields are a main part of the Solr schema, which provides major information to Solr while indexing. For our `musicCatalogue` example, we'll define the following fields:

```
<!-- Unique SongID -->
  <field name="songId" type="string" indexed="true" stored="true"
    required="true" multiValued="false"/>

  <!-- Song name -->
  <field name="songName" type="string" indexed="true"
    stored="true" required="true" multiValued="false" />

  <!-- Artist name -->
  <field name="artistName" type="string" indexed="true"
    stored="true" required="true" multiValued="false"/>

  <!-- Album Artist -->
  <field name="albumArtist" type="string" indexed="true"
    stored="true" required="false" multiValued="false"/>

  <!-- Album name -->
  <field name="albumName" type="string" indexed="true"
    stored="true" required="true" multiValued="false"/>

  <!-- Duration of the Song -->
  <field name="songDuration" type="double" indexed="true"
    stored="true" required="false" multiValued="false"/>
```

```
<!-- Duration of the Song -->
<field name="composer" type="string" indexed="true"
  stored="true" required="false" multiValued="false"/>


<!-- Song rating -->
<field name="rating" type="float" indexed="true" stored="true"
  required="false" default="0.0" multiValued="false"/>


<!-- Year which the song has been published -->
<field name="year" type="int" indexed="true" stored="true"
  required="false" multiValued="false"/>


<!-- Genre of the song (e.g. rock, pop, indie, etc)-->
<field name="genre" type="string" indexed="true" stored="true"
  required="false" multiValued="false"/>


<!-- Temporary field for storing all the information -->
<field name="tmpField" type="string" indexed="true"
  stored="true" required="false" multiValued="true"/>
```

The preceding fields, which we have defined, contain the following attributes:

- `name`: This denotes the name of the field
- `type`: This is the field type that we set up in the previous section
- `indexed`: Whether the field should be indexed by Solr or not (true or false)
- `required`: The `required` attribute tells Solr that when we're indexing the document, this field should be mandatory
- `multivalued`: If this is set to `true`, a document can contain multiple values of the same field
- `default`: This is the default value that should be used if there is no value available in the document
- `stored`: This field tells Solr to index the given field if the stored is set to `true`

Defining an unique key

A unique key element helps Solr maintain documents in a consistent way. This is an optional field and can be used as per the indexing requirements. If we think that the data that we feed into Solr will never come across as a duplicate document, we can avoid using this element.

The `uniqueKey` element can help us maintain a similar set of data. The format is as follows:

```
<uniqueKey>songId</uniqueKey>
```

Here, `songId` is a `uniqueKey`; it will be held in Solr just like a primary key in a database.

Copy fields and dynamic fields

A copy field tells Solr to copy the source field to the destination. This feature of Solr can be useful if we want to merge inputs of different elements into a single field. The following is the format by which we can introduce a `copyField` element in the schema:

```
<copyField source="sourceElement" destination="destinationElement"
/>
```

We can also merge all input fields into a single field using the ＊ symbol in the `source` attribute. This will merge all the fields into a single destination field, like this for example:

```
<copyField source="*" dest="result"/>
```

Dynamic copy fields can also be created in Solr using the following format:

```
<copyField source="*_t" dest="*_copyField"/>
```

So, suppose we're sending a field called `album_name_t`. Solr will dynamically create a new field called `album_name_t_copyField`.

Dynamic fields can be used in Solr where we don't have to define all the fields in `schema.xml`. For example, the following line of code tells Solr to create a dynamic field of the `string` type whenever it sees a field name ending with `_txt`:

```
<dynamicField name="*_txt" type="string" indexed="true"
store="true"/>
```

Building our musicCatalogue example

In our previous section, we saw how we can create a Solr schema using different fields and field types. Now let's use this schema to create a working Solr example.

To do this, we'll need to follow these steps:

1. As we've already created the folder structure required for our musicCatalogue example to work, let's go ahead and create the solrconfig.xml config file.

    The solrconfig.xml looks like the following:

    ```xml
    <?xml version="1.0" encoding="UTF-8" ?>
    <config>
      <luceneMatchVersion>4.10.1</luceneMatchVersion>
      <dataDir>${solr.data.dir:}</dataDir>

      <requestDispatcher handleSelect="false">
        <httpCaching never304="true"/>
      </requestDispatcher>
      <requestHandler name="/select" class="solr.SearchHandler"
        />
      <requestHandler name="/update"
        class="solr.UpdateRequestHandler"/>
      <requestHandler name="/admin"
        class="solr.admin.AdminHandlers"/>
    </config>
    ```

2. After we have created solrconfig.xml, we need to update solr.xml to add our musicCatalgoue core to it:

    ```xml
    <solr persistent="false">

    <cores adminPath="/admin/cores" defaultCoreName="collection1">
        <core name="collection1" instanceDir="collection1" />
        <core name="musicCatalog" instanceDir="musicCatalog"
          />
      </cores>
    </solr>
    ```

> In Solr 4.4 and above, a new feature has been introduced in Solr, called autoDiscovery. It automatically detects cores in the SOLR_HOME directory path.

3. Start the Solr server. After starting the Solr server, we can navigate to the Solr Admin UI (`http://localhost:8383/solr`).We'll see the following screen:

4. In the Solr Admin UI, we can navigate to our newly created `musicCatalog` core by selecting it from the drop-down list.

5. After going to the **musicCatalog** core, we can add some data into it by clicking on the **Document** tab and selecting **CSV** from the drop-down box. We can use the sample CSV file available in the book code file at `http://github.com/sachin-handiekar/SolrIndexingBook/Chapter-3` to populate the text field, and then click on **Submit Document**.

Using the Solr Admin UI

After we have inserted some data into Solr for indexing, we can use the query browser to see how Solr queries the indexed data.

We can use the Query Browser available in the Solr Admin UI to run our queries. In our `musicCatalogue` core, we can click on the **Query** tab to open the following window:

After opening this window, let's perform some queries on our recently added data, just to test whether our search query works or not. We'll simply use the default query and click on the **Execute Query** button. This will bring up all of the data that Solr has indexed in the musicCatalogue core.

When we open the **Query** tab, we can see that Solr has automatically selected the /select search handler for us, as shown here:

When we click on the **Execute Query** button, Solr will use the /`select` handler and perform the `*:*` query on it. The `*:*` query tells Solr to give us all the results, as the syntax of the query is [`field-name`]:[`value`], and the wildcard character (`*`) will give us all the results. This results in bringing forth all of the data that has been indexed. The following image shows the Solr Query Browser UI with the result and the query field populated:

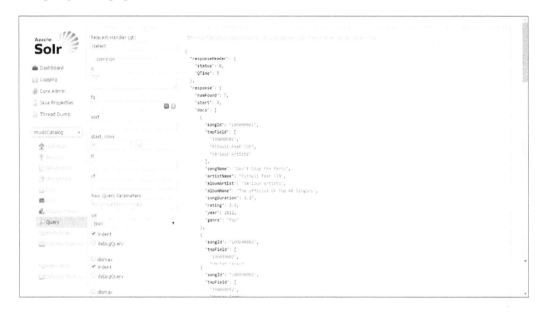

We can also use a direct URL to query the Solr Index, which will be helpful if we're using an API to get the indexed data. This link is also available above the search results on the Query browser:

```
http://localhost:8983/solr/musicCatalog/select?q=*%3A*&wt=json&indent
=true
```

Let's modify the `search` parameters and search for a song with a specific search criteria. To do this, let's go back the query browser and modify the search criteria.

After changing the query q parameter to `artistName:P*`, we tell Solr to get retrieve all the songs for which `artistName` starts with the letter "P" by passing a wildcard character (*). Moreover, after we execute this query, we'll get the following result:

```
{
  "responseHeader": {
    "status": 0,
    "QTime": 0
  },
  "response": {
    "numFound": 1,
    "start": 0,
    "docs": [
      {
        "songId": "100000001",
        "tmpField": [
          "100000001",
          "Pitbull Feat TJR",
          "Various Artists"
        ],
        "songName": "Don't Stop the Party",
        "artistName": "Pitbull Feat TJR",
        "albumArtist": "Various Artists",
        "albumName": "The official UK Top 40 Singles",
        "songDuration": 3.27,
        "rating": 3.5,
        "year": 2012,
        "genre": "Pop"
      }
    ]
  }
}
```

Then, after performing this query, let's see one more special feature provided by Solr, called faceting.

Facet searching

In Solr, a facet provides us with a way to arrange the result into categories based on the index terms. For example, in our `musicCatalogue`, we can arrange the songs based on genre (for example, rock, pop, world music, and so on). This feature is very helpful in e-commerce websites, where we need to see data in a categorical way. Let's see how we can enable faceting in our search queries. There are no special settings needed to get faceting to work in our `musicCatalogue` example.

Let's open the query browser tab for our musicCatalgoue example from the Solr Admin UI. This time, in the query input fields, we'll enable the facet checkbox and input the genre field in the facet.field textbox, like this:

After clicking on **Execute Query**, we can see the following JSON output, which will contain a special JSON element. This element will contain facet_counts:

```
"facet_counts": {
    "facet_queries": {},
    "facet_fields": {
      "genre": [
        "Pop",
        3,
        "Dance/Electronic",
        2,
        "Hip-Hop,Rap",
        1,
        "R&B,Soul",
        1
      ]
    },
    "facet_dates": {},
    "facet_ranges": {},
    "facet_intervals": {}
}
```

As we can see from the preceding JSON output, the genre facet element contains the group counts for the music that is indexed in Solr. The output that we've obtained can help users in performing better search queries.

Summary

In this chapter, we saw how we can create a schema from scratch and how Solr provides us with different functionalities. We can add these to our schema to help us achieve better search results.

We also created a schema for storing a music catalog and performed custom queries on it. These showed us a real-life example of how we can index data and get information back from Solr.

In the next chapter, we'll see how we can use the different index handlers provided by Solr to import our existing data.

4

Indexing Data – The Basic Technique and Using Index Handlers

In the previous chapter, we saw how Solr provides us with a way to index data using a schema. This chapter will cover techniques that can be used to index data in Solr. There are many ways of sending data to Solr using API or by making a POST call to update handlers. We'll cover the following topics in this chapter:

- Inserting data into Solr using basic POST tools
- Using XML and JSON handlers

Inserting data into Solr

Solr provides an easy-to-use command-line tool for sending data in various formats to the Solr server. We can use the post.jar or post.sh tool to send data to the Solr server to index data. Both of these tools are located in %SOLR_HOME%/example/exampledocs in the default installation folder.

 To see the commands for Solr 5.x, visit the Solr Wiki (https://wiki.apache.org/solr/).

We'll copy the two files (post.sh and post.jar) to the %SOLR_HOME/bin folder. The post.sh is a Unix shell script that wraps around the cURL command to send data to the Solr server. For Windows users, Solr has provided a standalone Java application packaged in a JAR format. It can be used in a way similar to the post.sh tool.

To run `post.jar`, open **Command Prompt** in Windows and enter the following:

```
$ %SOLR_HOME%/bin>java -jar post.jar -h
```

The result obtained by executing the preceding commands is as follows:

```
SimplePostTool version 1.5
Usage: java [SystemProperties] -jar post.jar [-h|-]
[<file|folder|url|arg> [<file|folder|url|arg>...]]

Supported System Properties and their defaults:
  -Ddata=files|web|args|stdin (default=files)
  -Dtype=<content-type> (default=application/xml)
  -Durl=<solr-update-url> (default=http://localhost:8983/solr/update)
  -Dauto=yes|no (default=no)
  -Drecursive=yes|no|<depth> (default=0)
  -Ddelay=<seconds> (default=0 for files, 10 for web)
  -Dfiletypes=<type>[,<type>,...] (default=xml,json,csv,pdf,doc,docx,
ppt,pptx,xl
s,xlsx,odt,odp,ods,ott,otp,ots,rtf,htm,html,txt,log)
  -Dparams="<key>=<value>[&<key>=<value>...]" (values must be URL-
    encoded)
  -Dcommit=yes|no (default=yes)
  -Doptimize=yes|no (default=no)
  -Dout=yes|no (default=no)
```

Let's test the `post.jar` utility by sending a JSON document to our Solr server. We'll feed some data to the `musicCatalogue` example, which we created in *Chapter 3, Indexing Data*. The sample files are available in this chapter code base, which can be used to feed the data into the Solr instance.

For sending this JSON data, we'll execute the following command from the examples' directory that comes with this book. We're specifying the `-Durl` system property, which will refer to our `musicCatalog` core:

```
$ java -Durl="http://localhost:8983/solr/musicCatalog/update"
-Dtype=application/json -jar %SOLR_HOME%/post.jar %SOLR_INDEXING_EXAMPLE/
Chapter-4/sampleMusic.json

SimplePostTool version 1.5
Posting files to base url http://localhost:8983/solr/musicCatalog/update
using content-type application/json..
POSTing file sampleMusic.json
1 files indexed.
COMMITting Solr index changes to http://localhost:8983/solr/musicCatalog/
update.
.
Time spent: 0:00:00.150
```

Note that we're assuming that you have set the SOLR_HOME path to the Solr installation directory.

After we have executed this command, we can go to the query browser window from the Solr admin UI console and see that the data gets indexed in our musicCatalogue example. We've added a song with the songName attribute set to "Yo (Excuse Me Miss)" and the artistName attribute set to Chris Brown. We can execute the following query to see the newly inserted data:

```
q = songName:Yo*
```

The following screenshot shows the data that is returned after we perform the query:

As we can see from the preceding screenshot, the Solr query browser has returned us a document that was indexed after running the post.jar utility tool.

The next important topic in indexing data in Solr is the use of request handlers that come with Solr. Request handlers in Solr provide us with a way to add, delete, update, and search for documents in the Solr Index.

Solr comes with a lot of plugins that can be used to import documents from a large number of sources. Documents can be indexed using Apache Tika—you can index documents such as MS Word documents, Excel spreadsheets, PDF documents, and many more file formats.

Also, Solr provides us with a way to import data from relational databases or structured data types using the data import handler. We'll see how we can use the data import handler in *Chapter 5, Index Data Using Structured Datasources Using DIH*, where we'll cover this in detail.

By default, Solr provides a way to index structured documents in XML, CSV, and JSON documents. In the following section, we'll see how we can use the request handlers provided by Solr to import these documents.

Request handlers can be mapped in the following two ways:

- Path-based names, which can be specified in the URL
- Using the qt (query-type) parameter

A request handler can be used to support different data types using the content-type parameter.

Configuring UpdateRequestHandler

In *Chapter 3, Indexing Data*, we created a Solr configuration file, and we'll be reusing it to add a request handler.

In solrconfig.xml, we've added the following line to add a request handler of the solr.UpdateRequestHandler type, which will be mapped to the /update url path. This handler will tell Solr that /update will be used to receive commands/documents that will be used by UpdateRequestHandler:

```
<requestHandler name="/update" class="solr.UpdateRequestHandler"
/>
```

Indexing documents using XML

In Solr, we can index XML messages to the update handler using the content-type tag: for example application/xml or text/xml. In the following subsections, we'll see how we can perform add, update, or delete commands.

Adding and updating documents

Solr provides an easy-to-use XML schema; this schema can be used to index data in Solr. The XML schema mainly contains the following elements:

- <add>: This element is the parent element, and it tells Solr that we're adding a document for indexing

- `<doc>`: This element contains all the fields that are going to be indexed
- `<field>`: This element contains the content, name, and value of the field that is going to be indexed

For example, the sample XML document looks like the following code:

```
<add>
  <doc>
    <field name="songId">100000010</field>
    <field name="songName">(Oh No) What You Got</field>
    <field name="artistName">Justin Timberlake</field>
    <field name="albumArtist">Various</field>
    <field name="albumName">Justified</field>
    <field name="songDuration">4.31</field>
    <field name="composer"></field>
    <field name="rating"></field>
    <field name="year">2002</field>
    <field name="genre">Pop, Teen Pop</field>
  </doc>
</add>
```

Every element contains optional attributes, which can be used to further optimize the indexing process. The following is an example of such an optional attribute that can be used:

```
<add overwrite="false">
  <doc boost="1.5">
    <field name="songId">100000010</field>
    <field name="songName">(Oh No) What You Got</field>
    <field name="artistName">Justin Timberlake</field>
    /* More fields */
  </doc>
</add>
```

In the preceding example, we can see that the `<add>` element accepts an optional attribute named overwrite, which is set to `true` by default. This element will overwrite the indexed data if the unique key of the document is already indexed in Solr.

The `boost` attribute, on the other hand, provides a unique way of increasing the score of a document. This attribute can be applied to both `<doc>` and `<field>` elements. In addition to the `boost` attribute, the `<field>` element also contains an attribute named `update`, which we'll discuss in *Chapter 8, Commits, Real-time Index Optimizations, and Atomic Updates.*

Deleting a document

An indexed document in Solr can be deleted by sending an XML message to the `/update` handler. Documents can be deleted from Solr in the following two ways:

- `By ID`: Documents can be deleted from Solr by unique ID, which can be used only if the uniqueID field is present in the schema:

  ```
  <delete>
  <id>100000010</id>
   </delete>
  ```

- `By query`: Documents can also be deleted from Solr by using a query to delete a range of documents:

  ```
  <delete>
  <query>albumName:Justified</query>
   </delete>
  ```

The following is an example of combining both an ID and a query in a `<delete>` XML message:

```
<delete>
<id>100000010</id>
<query>albumName:Justified</query>
</delete>
```

We can use the `POST.jar` tool or `post.sh` to send delete XML messages to Solr. Here is an example of using the `POST.jar` tool:

```
$ java -Ddata=args
-Durl="http://localhost:8983/solr/musicCatalog/update"
-jar %SOLR_HOME%/post.jar "<delete><id>100000010</
id><query>albumName:Justified</query></delete>"
```

We can also send XML messages to the Solr server using cURL. We can use the `data-binary` option to append XML messages while making a HTTP POST request to Solr:

 Note that Windows users can also download cURL for Windows from `http://curl.haxx.se/`, or install it in Cygwin.

```
$ curl http://localhost:8983/solr/musicCatalog/update -H "Content-
Type: text/xml" --data-binary '<add>
  <doc>
    <field name="songId">100000010</field>
    <field name="songName">(Oh No) What You Got</field>
    <field name="artistName">Justin Timberlake</field>
```

```
    <field name="albumArtist">Various</field>
    <field name="albumName">Justified</field>
    <field name="songDuration">4.31</field>
    <field name="composer"></field>
    <field name="rating">3.4</field>
    <field name="year">2002</field>
    <field name="genre">Pop</field>
  </doc>
</add>'
```

We can also send the contents of an XML file to Solr using the following cURL command:

```
$ curl http://localhost:8983/solr/musicCatalog/update -H "Content-
Type: text/xml" --data-binary @sampleData.xml
```

If all goes well, the Solr server will return an XML response to us. The following is what we can expect from Solr if all goes well:

```
<?xml version="1.0" encoding="UTF-8"?>
<response>
  <lst name="responseHeader">
    <int name="status">0</int>
    <int name="QTime">0</int>
  </lst>
</response>
```

The Solr response element consists of a child element, which contains responseHeader. The responseHeader element itself contains two child elements; they contain the status and the QTime element. The default status is set to 0 in Solr, and QTime tells the processing time of a request to the server in milliseconds.

Indexing documents using JSON

In the previous section, we saw how we can add, update, and delete documents using XML. In this section, we'll see how we can perform the same operations using JSON data types.

We can send the JSON-formatted update request using Solr's update handler, by setting Content-type: application/json or text/json. There are three basic types of JSON documents that can be sent to Solr. They are:

- A single document
- A list of documents — an array of documents
- A sequence of updated documents — a map type object that contains multiple commands

Adding a single document

We can add a single JSON document to Solr by posting the data to the /update/ json/docs handler path. The following is an example of indexing JSON data in Solr:

```
$ curl 'http://localhost:8983/solr/musicCatalog/update/json/docs'
-H 'Content-Type: application/json'  --data-binary '
{
    "songId":100000006,
    "songName":"Fester Skank (feat. Diztortion)",
    "artistName":"Lethal Bizzle",
    "albumArtist":"",
    "albumName":"The Official UK Top 10 Singles",
    "songDuration":2.25,
    "composer":"",
    "rating":4,
    "year":2015,
    "genre":"Hip-Hop,Rap"
}'
```

Adding multiple JSON documents

Similar to adding a single JSON document, we can add multiple JSON documents using a JSON array type structure that consists of JSON objects. Here is an example of sending multiple JSON documents to Solr for indexing:

```
$ curl -X POST -H 'Content-Type: application/json' 'http://
localhost:8983/solr/musicCatalog/update' --data-binary '
  [
   {
    "songId":100000006,
    "songName":"Fester Skank (feat. Diztortion)",
    "artistName":"Lethal Bizzle",
    "albumArtist":"",
    "albumName":"The Official UK Top 10 Singles",
    "songDuration":2.25,
    "composer":"",
    "rating":4,
    "year":2015,
    "genre":"Hip-Hop,Rap"
   },
   {
    "songId":100000007,
    "songName":"Yo (Excuse Me Miss)",
```

```
        "artistName":"Chris Brown",
        "albumArtist":"",
        "albumName":"The Official UK Top 10 Singles",
        "songDuration":3.49,
        "composer":"",
        "rating":4.5,
        "year":2006,
        "genre":"R&B,Soul"
    }
]'
```

A sample JSON file is provided at `$SOLR_EXAMPLES/Chapter-4/sampleMusic.`
`json`, and it contains an array of objects that we can add to the Solr `musicCatalog`
example:

```
$ curl 'http://localhost:8983/solr/musicCatalog/update?commit=true'
--data-binary @sampleMusic.json -H 'Content-type:application/json'
```

Sequential JSON update commands

We can also send multiple JSON `update` commands, such as add, delete, and
commit, within a single JSON document to Solr for indexing. The JSON `update`
command is able to support multiple commands at once. The following is an
example of sending multiple JSON commands:

```
curl -X POST -H 'Content-Type: application/json' 'http://
localhost:8983/solr/musicCatalog/update' --data-binary '
{
  "add": {
    "doc": {
    "songId":100000006,
    "songName":"Fester Skank (feat. Diztortion)",
    "artistName":"Lethal Bizzle",
    "albumArtist":"",
    "albumName":"The Official UK Top 10 Singles",
    "songDuration":2.25,
    "composer":"",
    "rating":4,
    "year":2015,
    "genre":"Hip-Hop,Rap"
    }
  },
  "commit": {},
  "delete": { "query":"albumName:Justified" },
  "delete": { "id":"100000006" }
}'
```

As seen from this example, we're passing multiple commands—add, commit, and delete—within a single JSON document. The delete command can accept both the query and the ID to remove data from Solr. Here is an example of deleting multiple IDs from Solr:

```
{ "delete":"id1" }
```

Another one is as follows:

```
{"delete":["id1","id2"]  }
```

Indexing updates using CSV

At last, we'll now see how we can index CSV data in Solr using Content-Type: text/csv. A sample CSV file has been provided at %SOLR_EXAMPLES/Chapter-4/ sampleMusicCatalog.csv, and we can use it to add documents to our musicCatalgoue example.

The following is an example of indexing data using the curl command:

```
curl 'http://localhost:8983/solr/musicCatalog/update' --data-binary @
sampleMusicCatalog.csv -H 'Content-type:application/csv'
```

In the preceding command, we're telling CSVUpdateHandler to use the first line of the CSV as the header row, which will contain the field name. If the CSV does not have a header row, we can use the header=false parameter, which will tell UpdateHandler that there is no header row present. We can specify the field names in the CSV using another parameter named fieldnames, which accepts a comma-separated list of field names for the CSV file. There are a lot of optional configurations that can be set on the update handler. More information is available at https://wiki.apache.org/solr/ UpdateCSV.

We can also index tab-delimited files in Solr by setting the separator parameter to tab (%09) and escape parameter to backslash (%5C) in the URL. Here is an example of indexing tab-delimited files in Solr:

```
$ curl
'http://localhost:8983/solr/update/csv?commit=true&separator=%09&escape=%
5c' --data-binary @tabSeparatedMusicCatalog.csv
```

Summary

In this chapter, we saw how we can use the different index handlers. With these, we can index data using XML, JSON, and CSV data to Solr. We also saw how we can use tools such as post.jar and post.sh, which come with the default Solr installation, to send documents to Solr for adding, updating, and deleting documents from the Solr index.

In the next chapter, we'll see how we can use the data import handler provided by Solr to import data from relational databases and feed it into Solr.

5
Indexing Data with the Help of Structured Datasources – Using DIH

In the previous chapter, we saw how we can index data using the XML, JSON, and CSV update handlers provided by Solr. In this chapter, we'll see how we can import data from a data store (for example, a database, XML that uses XPath, and many more) using the inbuilt functionalities of Solr. We'll cover the following topics:

* Configuring a custom datasource for our data import handler
* The various datasources available in Solr
* Customization of the data import handler

Indexing data from MySQL

In this section, we'll see how we can set up a MySQL database in Solr to index our data from the database to Solr directly. To do this, we'll use the `musicCatalog` schema, which we developed in previous chapters, and we will create a similar table to hold the data in the MySQL database.

Configuring datasource

We're assuming that you already have a MySQL database running on your machine. In the MySQL database, we'll need to create the following table to hold the `musicCatalogue` data.

Let's go ahead and create a database called `solrIndexingExample` in MySQL. We can use the following SQL to create a new database:

```
create database solrIndexingExample;

use solrIndexingExample;
```

After we have created the database, we'll need to create a table that will hold our data for musicCatalog. We can use this SQL query to create a table:

```
CREATE TABLE musiccatalog (
    songId int(11) NOT NULL AUTO_INCREMENT,
    songName varchar(250) DEFAULT NULL,
    artistName varchar(250) DEFAULT NULL,
    albumArtist varchar(150) DEFAULT NULL,
    albumName varchar(150) DEFAULT NULL,
    songDuration double DEFAULT NULL,
    composer varchar(50) DEFAULT NULL,
    rating float DEFAULT NULL,
    year int(11) DEFAULT NULL,
    genre varchar(100) DEFAULT NULL,
    PRIMARY KEY (songId)
)
```

The SQL script for creating the table and inserting sample data is available in the Chapter 5 code provided with this book.

After setting up the table with some sample data, we can move on to setting the Solr configuration, which will communicate with to the MySQL database.

We'll need to perform the following steps to set up MySQL for our Solr instance:

1. Download and copy the MySQL JDBC driver from the https://dev.mysql.com/downloads/connector/j/ into $SOLR_HOME/dist folder.

2. Create a new core named musicCatalogue-DIH in %SOLR_HOME/examples/ with the following directory structure type. Alternatively, we can copy the core from the Chapter 5 code provided with this book:

```
musicCatalog-DIH
        |-- conf
        |-- schema.xml
        |-- db-data-config.xml
        |-- solrconfig.xml
```

3. Add `solr-datamporthandler.jar` and the MySQL driver using the `lib` tag in `solrconfig.xml`:

```
<!-- Solr DataImportHandler -->
    <lib dir="../../../dist/" regex="solr-
       dataimporthandler-.*\.jar"/>
    <lib dir="../../../dist/" regex="solr-
       dataimporthandler-extras-\d.*\.jar"/>

       <!-- MySQL Driver -->
   <lib dir="../../../dist/" regex="mysql-connector-java-\d.*\.
jar"/>
```

Add the request handler (solr.DataImportHandler)

```
<requestHandler name="/dataimport"
  class="solr.DataImportHandler">
  <lst name="defaults">
     <str name="config">db-data-config.xml</str>
  </lst>
</requestHandler>
```

4. Next, add `db-data-config.xml` to the `conf` folder which is in the `musicCatalogue-DIH` core folder:

```
<dataConfig>
  <dataSource name="mysqlDS"

     driver="com.mysql.jdbc.Driver"

     url="jdbc:mysql://localhost:3306/
        solrIndexingExample"

     user="<username>"

     password="<password>"/>

  <document>
    <entity name="musicCatalog" query="select * from
    musicCatalog">
    <field column="songId" name="songId"/>
    <field column="songName" name="songName"/>
    <field column="aristName" name="artistName"/>
    <field column="albumArtist" name="albumArtist"/>
    <field column="albumName" name="albumName"/>
    <field column="songDuration" name="songDuration"/>
```

```
                <field column="composer" name="composer"/>
                <field column="rating" name="rating"/>
                <field column="year" name="year"/>
                <field column="genre" name="genre"/>
            </entity>
        </document>
    </dataConfig>
```

As of now, we've configured our core to communicate with to the MySQL database. Let's go into the details of what we've configured so far. The `db-data-config.xml` file contains the datasource element that we've configured for the MySQL database, and it also contains the user credentials and the `jdbc` URL for connecting Solr to the MySQL database. The default datasource type, if not specified, is `JDBCDataSource`, which is needed in our scenario. This is because we're using the MySQL JDBC driver for the connection. Here is an example of the datasource config:

```
<dataSource name="mysqlDS"
        driver="com.mysql.jdbc.Driver"

        url="jdbc:mysql://localhost:3306/solrIndexingExample"

        user="<username>"

        password="<password>"/>
```

After configuring the datasource element, we have to create a document element that will hold the entity element and field elements, which are going to map with the database entity. In `db-data-config.xml`, we specify the following entity for `musicCatalog`:

```
<entity name="musicCatalog" query="select * from musicCatalog">
```

By default, `SQLEntityProcessor` is used by `JDBCDataSource`. Database columns can be mapped to Solr fields using the `field` element, like this for example:

```
<field column="songId" name="songId" />
```

The `column` attribute holds the database column name and the `name` attribute holds the relevant Solr field name.

After completing the setup, we can navigate to our newly added `musicCatalogue-DIH` core from `http://localhost:8983/solr/`, and click on the **DataImport** tab. As we've added a request handler in our `solrconfig.xml` configuration file, the **DataImport** tab that was previously disabled gets automatically enabled by Solr.

As we can see from the following screenshot, we can perform various operations on our new data import handler.

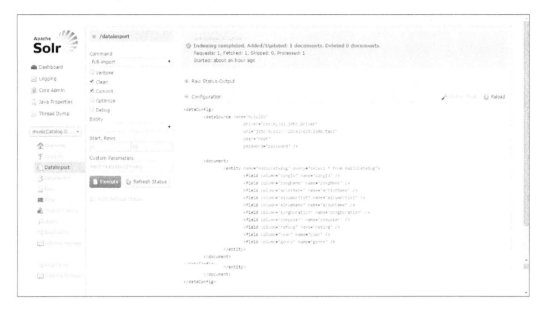

DIH commands

Let's run some commands over our newly created datasource and see what functionalities Solr provides for us:

- **Delta import**: This command is used to import incremental or new changes from the data store to Solr. Here is an example: `http://localhost:8983/solr/musicCatalog-DIH/dataimport?command=delta-import`.

- **Full import**: This command is used to index all the rows of a table in the database into Solr. The following is an example: `http://localhost:8983/solr/musicCatalog-DIH/dataimport?command=full-import`.

- **Reloading configuration**: This command is used to reload the `db-data-config.xml` file if there are changes made to it after Solr has been started. This is an example: `http://localhost:8983/solr/musicCatalog-DIH/dataimport?command=reload-config`.

- **Checking status**: This command is used to check the status of an import that we've performed, for example: `http://localhost:8983/solr/musicCatalog-DIH/dataimport?command=status`.

- **Aborting the current import**: The `abort` command is used to cancel the current import, which is being done on the core, for example: `http://localhost:8983/solr/musicCatalog-DIH/dataimport?command=abort`.

The preceding commands, which we've just discussed, will result in the following XML response from Solr:

```xml
<?xml version="1.0" encoding="UTF-8"?>
<response>
    <lst name="responseHeader">
      <int name="status">0</int>
      <int name="QTime">20</int>
    </lst>
    <lst name="initArgs">
      <lst name="defaults">
        <str name="config">db-data-config.xml</str>
      </lst>
    </lst>
    <str name="command">full-import</str>
    <str name="status">idle</str>
    <str name="importResponse"/>
    <lst name="statusMessages">
      <str name="Total Requests made to DataSource">1</str>
      <str name="Total Rows Fetched">1</str>
      <str name="Total Documents Skipped">0</str>
      <str name="Full Dump Started">2015-08-12 08:48:25</str>
      <str name="">Indexing completed. Added/Updated: 1 documents.
        Deleted 0 documents.</str>
      <str name="Committed">2015-08-12 08:48:25</str>
      <str name="Total Documents Processed">1</str>
      <str name="Time taken">0:0:0.274</str>
    </lst>
    <str name="WARNING">This response format is experimental.  It
      is likely to change in the future.</str>
</response>
```

There are also some optional attributes that we can use with the preceding commands. We won't be covering them in this chapter, but they can be checked out in the Solr documentation at `https://wiki.apache.org/solr/DataImportHandler#Commands`.

So now, we've seen how we can import data into Solr from a MySQL database. Next, let's see how we can use other datasources (for example, FileDataSource, URLDataSource, and many more).

Indexing data using XPath

For simplicity, we'll use FileDataSource. With it, we can import data into Solr from XML files using XPathEntityProcessor to retrieve the data.

Let's go ahead and create a new core named MusicCatalogue-DIH-XPath in Solr. We can create the configuration files similarly to the ones we previously created for JDBCDataSource.

In solrconfig.xml, we'll use the following content:

```
<requestHandler name="/dataimport"
  class="solr.DataImportHandler">
  <lst name="defaults">
    <str name="config">xpath-data-config.xml</str>
  </lst>
</requestHandler>
```

We'll create a new file called xpath-data-config.xml, which will contain FileDataSource and XPathEntityProcessor:

```
<dataConfig>
  <!-- File Data Source -->
  <dataSource type="FileDataSource" encoding="UTF-8" />

  <document>
    <entity
      processor="XPathEntityProcessor"
      name="musicCatalog"
      pk="songId"
      url="/path/to/SolrIndexingExamples/Chapter-5/sampleData.xml"
      forEach="/musicCatalog/albums/album/"
      transformer="RegexTransformer">

      <field column="songId"
        xpath="/musicCatalog/albums/album/songId"/>
      <field column="songName"
        xpath="/musicCatalog/albums/album/songName"/>
      <field column="artistName"
        xpath="/musicCatalog/albums/album/artistName"/>
```

```
        <field column="albumArtist"
          xpath="/musicCatalog/albums/album/albumArtist"/>
        <field column="albumName"
          xpath="/musicCatalog/albums/album/albumName"/>
        <field column="songDuration"
          xpath="/musicCatalog/albums/album/songDuration"/>
        <field column="composer"
          xpath="/musicCatalog/albums/album/composer"/>
        <field column="rating"
          xpath="/musicCatalog/albums/album/rating"/>
        <field column="year"
          xpath="/musicCatalog/albums/album/year"/>
        <field column="genre"
          xpath="/musicCatalog/albums/album/genre"/>
      </entity>
    </document>
  </dataConfig>
```

In the preceding `<dataConfig>` element, we're just using a single XML file; we need to get this file indexed for our example. We can also use the following configuration to index a list of XML files:

```
<dataConfig>
  <dataSource type="FileDataSource" encoding="UTF-8"/>
  <document>
    <entity
      name="document"
      processor="FileListEntityProcessor"
      baseDir="/path/to/xml-files"
      fileName=".*\.xml$"
      recursive="false"
      rootEntity="false"
      dataSource="null">
      <entity
      processor="XPathEntityProcessor"
      name="musicCatalog"
      pk="songId"
      url="${document.fileAbsolutePath}"
      forEach="/musicCatalog/albums/album/"
      transformer="RegexTransformer">

      <!-- Definition of Fields as per the previous example -->
      </entity>
    </entity>
  </document>
</dataConfig>
```

A sample XML file that contains the sample album data has been provided in the code that is available with this book.

The contents of the sample XML file look like the following:

```
<musicCatalog>
  <albums>
    <album>
      <songId>100000010</songId>
      <songName>(Oh No) What You Got</songName>
      <artistName>Justin Timberlake</artistName>
      <albumArtist>Various</albumArtist>
      <albumName>Justified</albumName>
      <songDuration>4.31</songDuration>
      <composer/>
      <rating>3.5</rating>
      <year>2002</year>
      <genre>Pop, Electronic, Dance, Adult Contemporary, Teen
        Pop</genre>
    </album>
  </albums>
</musicCatalog>
```

As we can see from `xpath-data-config.xml`, we are using `FileDataSource` to read the contents of the file. Then, using `XPathEntityProcessor`, we fetch the values of the field. For example, we retrieve `artistName` using the following code:

```
<field column="artistName"
xpath="/musicCatalog/albums/album/artistName"/>
```

The `xpath` attribute is used to pass an XPath expression to the field element, which is used by `XPathEntityProcessor` to retrieve the `artistName` value from the XML document and is then fed into Solr for indexing.

Let's test our newly created core in Solr. To do this, we'll start our Solr instance and navigate to the Solr Admin UI (`http://localhost:8983/solr/#/musicCatalog-DIH-XPath/`).

Let's import the XML data using the **DataImport** tab. To do this, click on the **Dataimport** tab, select the **full-import** option, and click on **Execute**, as shown in this screenshot:

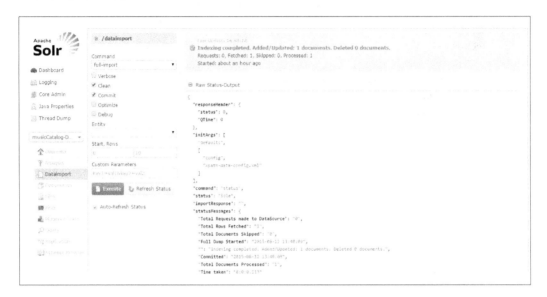

As we can see from the preceding screenshot, after we click on the **Execute** button, the data import handler indexes the data from the XML file into Solr. Solr gives the following output, which tells the user how many documents were added/updated or deleted:

Last Update: 14:51:25
Indexing completed. Added/Updated: 1 documents. Deleted 0 documents.
Requests: 0, Fetched: 1, Skipped: 0, Processed: 1
Started: about an hour ago

After running the import, we can query the Solr index to retrieve our indexed document. To do this, we can use the query browser in the Solr Admin UI, or we can directly go to this URL:

```
http://localhost:8983/solr/musicCatalog-DIH-XPath/select?q=*%3A*&wt=j
son&indent=true
```

The following result is expected if the data import is successful:

```
{
    "responseHeader":{
        "status":0,
        "QTime":0
```

```
    },
    "response":{
      "numFound":1,
      "start":0,
      "docs":[
        {
            "genre":"Pop, Electronic, Dance, Adult Contemporary,
              Teen Pop",
            "composer":"",
            "albumArtist":"Various",
            "tmpField":[
               "Various",
               "100000010",
               "Justin Timberlake"
            ],
            "albumName":"Justified",
            "songDuration":4.31,
            "year":2002,
            "songName":"(Oh No) What You Got",
            "rating":3.5,
            "songId":"100000010",
            "artistName":"Justin Timberlake"
        }
      ]
    }
}
```

The preceding result shows us how we can use the data import handler to index XML documents into Solr.

Summary

In this chapter, we saw how we can use the data import handler provided by Solr to import data from various datasources. There are a lot of things that we did not cover in this chapter, and they are beyond the scope of this book, such as entity processors, transformers, and many more. You can read more about this advanced feature on the Solr Data Import Handler wiki (https://wiki.apache.org/solr/DataImportHandler).

In the next chapter, we'll see how we can extract data from various file formats, such as .doc, .ppt, .xls, and many more, and index it in Solr using Apache Tika.

6

Indexing Data Using Apache Tika

In previous chapters, we saw how we can use the data import handler provided by Solr to index data using various datasources (JDBC and file datasource). In this chapter, we'll see how we can index data for various file formats, such as MS Word, Excel, PDF and many more. We'll cover the following topics:

- Introducing Apache Tika
- Configuring Apache Tika in Solr
- Indexing PDF and Word documents

Introducing Apache Tika

Apache Tika is an open source library that is used for document type detection and content extraction from various file formats. It uses various existing document parsers and document type detection techniques to detect and extract data. Using Tika, we can develop a universal type detector and content extractor to extract both structured text as well as metadata from different types of documents such as spreadsheets, text documents, images, PDFs, and even multimedia input formats. Apache Tika provides a single API for parsing different file formats. The existing parser libraries are encapsulated under a single interface, called the **parser** interface.

Configuring Apache Tika in Solr

Let's go ahead and create a new core called **tika-example** in our Solr instance. To make things easier, you can copy the core from the Chapter 6 folder of the ZIP file that comes with this book. After creating the core, we'll need to configure solrconfig.xml.

We need to add the extraction libraries that are available in the %SOLR_HOME/ contrib/extraction/lib folder, and also the solr-cell library in solrconfig. xml:

```
<lib dir="${solr.install.dir:../../..}/contrib/extraction/lib"
regex=".*\.jar"/>
<lib dir="${solr.install.dir:../../..}/dist/" regex="solr-cell-\d.*\.
jar"/>
```

We can then configure ExtractingRequestHandler in solrconfig.xml:

```
<requestHandler name="/update/extract"
class="solr.extraction.ExtractingRequestHandler">
  <lst name="defaults">
    <str name="fmap.content">content</str>
    <str name="lowernames">true</str>
    <str name="uprefix">attr_</str>
    <str name="captureAttr">false</str>
  </lst>
</requestHandler>
```

We can override the default values used by ExtractingRequestHandler by passing it in the defaults list. ExtractingRequestHandler will, by default, put the content of the extracted file into the text field. But we can override that using fmap.content key. Also, captureAttr will tell ExtractingRequestHandler to get all the metadata information from the document. To keep this example simple, we'll set captureAttr to false.

The solrconfig.xml configuration file will look as follows:

```
<?xml version="1.0" encoding="UTF-8" ?>
<config>
  <luceneMatchVersion>4.10.1</luceneMatchVersion>
  <lib dir="../../../contrib/dataimporthandler/lib/"
    regex=".*\.jar"/>
  <lib dir="../../../dist/" regex="solr-dataimporthandler-.*\.jar"
    />

  <lib dir="../../../contrib/extraction/lib" regex=".*\.jar"/>
  <lib dir="../../../dist/" regex="solr-cell-\d.*\.jar"/>

  <dataDir>${solr.data.dir:}</dataDir>

  <requestDispatcher handleSelect="false">
    <httpCaching never304="true"/>
  </requestDispatcher>
```

```
<requestHandler name="/select" class="solr.SearchHandler"/>
<requestHandler name="/update" class="solr.UpdateRequestHandler"
  />
<requestHandler name="/admin" class="solr.admin.AdminHandlers"
  />
<requestHandler name="/analysis/field"
  class="solr.FieldAnalysisRequestHandler" startup="lazy"/>

<requestHandler name="/update/extract"
  class="solr.extraction.ExtractingRequestHandler">
  <lst name="defaults">
    <str name="fmap.content">content</str>
    <str name="lowernames">true</str>
    <str name="uprefix">attr_</str>
    <str name="captureAttr">false</str>
  </lst>
</requestHandler>
</config>
```

After making the configuration changes, let's go ahead and index some documents in Solr.

Indexing PDF and Word documents

We'll create a new schema that will hold the metadata information for our indexed files. Apache Tika will extract the metadata information from the file that we pass to it. The schema.xml configuration, which we'll use, looks like the following:

```
<?xml version="1.0" encoding="UTF-8" ?>
<schema name="tika-example" version="1.5">

  <field name="title" type="text_general" indexed="true"
    stored="true" multiValued="true"/>
  <field name="author" type="text_general" indexed="true"
    stored="true"/>
  <field name="content" type="text_general" indexed="true"
    stored="true" multiValued="true"/>

  <dynamicField name="attr_*" type="text_general" indexed="true"
    stored="false" multiValued="true"/>

  <fieldType name="text_general" class="solr.TextField"
    positionIncrementGap="100">
    <analyzer>
```

```
      <charFilter class="solr.PatternReplaceCharFilterFactory"
        pattern="([\\n])" replacement=""/>
      <tokenizer class="solr.StandardTokenizerFactory"/>
      <filter class="solr.LowerCaseFilterFactory"/>
    </analyzer>

  </fieldType>

</schema>
```

Let's now send a Word document to Solr for indexing. All the relevant code examples and sample files can be found in $SOLR_INDEXING_BOOK/Chapter06/tika-example.

We'll use the post.jar tool to index a Word document (.doc) to the Solr server:

```
$ java -Durl=http://localhost:8983/solr/tika-
example/update/extract?commit=true -Dtype=application/msword -jar
post.jar %SOLR_EXAMPLES/Chapter06/test-tika.docx
```

As we can see from the command, we're specifying the content-type of the file that we're indexing through -Dtype=application/msword. As we're sending a PDF file, we can use application/pdf as the content type.

After running the command, we will see the following output:

```
SimplePostTool version 1.5
Posting files to base url http://localhost:8983/solr/tika-
example/update/extract
  using content-type application/msword..
POSTing file test-tika.docx
1 files indexed.
COMMITting Solr index changes to http://localhost:8983/solr/tika-
example/update/
extract..
Time spent: 0:00:01.499
```

After we've indexed the sample Word document in index, we can use the Solr query browser to see how the document has been indexed in Solr. As we can see from the preceding screenshot, the Solr query returns the following indexed document, and the content inside the Word document is stored in the content field.

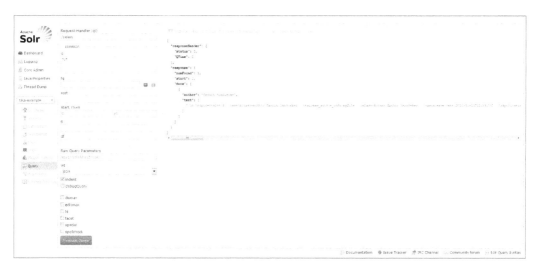

The `metadata` attributes are currently not stored in Solr while indexing the document. However, we can enable indexing for the metadata attribute by changing the dynamic attribute field in `schema.xml` to the following:

```
<dynamicField name="attr_*" type="text_general" indexed="true"
    stored="true" multiValued="true"/>
```

Summary

In this chapter, we saw how we can index files such as PDF, Word documents, and spreadsheets in Solr using the powerful features of Apache Tika. There are many more features available for use, but they are beyond the scope of this book. However, you can get a clear picture here on how easy it is to set up Apache Tika with Solr in order to retrieve information from a document. In the next chapter, we'll see how we can use Apache Nutch to crawl web pages and index the information received by the crawler in Solr.

7
Apache Nutch

In the previous chapter, we saw how we can index documents using Apache Tika into Solr. In this chapter, we'll see how we can use Apache Nutch to index web content into Solr and index them in Solr. This chapter will cover the following topics:

- Introducing to Apache Nutch
- Installing Apache Nutch
- Configuring Solr with Nutch

Introducing Apache Nutch

Apache Nutch is an open source web crawler that can be used to retrieve data from websites and get data from it. It is an extensible and scalable crawler that gives us the freedom to use it as we like by using plugins. Apache Nutch is written in Java, just like Apache Solr, and both tools make a perfect combination for creating a search engine of our own if they are combined.

Apache Nutch can be used on a single node or can be run in a distributed way with multiple nodes. Let's see how we can combine Apache Solr and Apache Nutch to crawl a web page and index it. To do this, let's start by installing Apache Nutch.

Installing Apache Nutch

Apache Nutch comes in two versions (1.x and 2.x). For this example, we'll be using version 1.x, as it contains a binary that will help reduce the time taken to build version 2.x from scratch. The latest stable version of Apache Nutch (v1.10), which also contains a binary at the time of writing this book, can be installed by following these steps:

1. Download and unzip Apache Nutch (`apache-nutch-1.10-bin.tar.gz`) from `http://nutch.apache.org/downloads.html`.

2. Extract the archive file into a folder of your choice. We'll use `%NUTCH_HOME%` as the folder where the ZIP file is to be extracted.

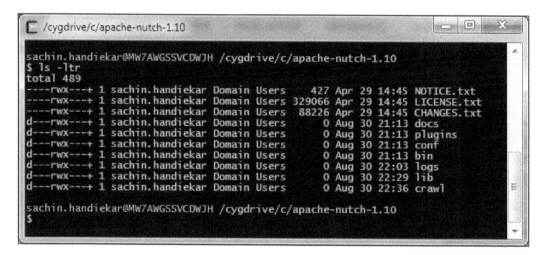

 On Windows, we can install Cygwin by going to the installation link at `http://cygwin.com/install.html`.

Let's verify the downloaded archive by going to `%NUTCH_HOME%/bin`. It will contain the `Nutch` script, which we can execute. We run the following command to get a list of available options that we can use:

```
$ cd %NUTCH_HOME%/bin
```

```
$ ./nutch
```

We should get the following output from the command:

```
Usage: nutch COMMAND
where COMMAND is one of:
inject          inject new urls into the database
hostinject      creates or updates an existing host table from a text file
generate        generate new batches to fetch from crawl db
fetch           fetch URLs marked during generate
parse           parse URLs marked during fetch
updatedb        update web table after parsing
updatehostdb    update host table after parsing
readdb          read/dump records from page database
readhostdb      display entries from the hostDB
index           run the plugin-based indexer on parsed batches
elasticindex    run the elasticsearch indexer - DEPRECATED use the index
                command instead
solrindex       run the solr indexer on parsed batches - DEPRECATED use
                the index command instead
solrdedup       remove duplicates from solr
solrclean       remove HTTP 301 and 404 documents from solr - DEPRECATED
                use the clean command instead
clean           remove HTTP 301 and 404 documents and duplicates from
                indexing backends configured via plugins
parsechecker    check the parser for a given url
indexchecker    check the indexing filters for a given url
plugin          load a plugin and run one of its classes main()
nutchserver     run a (local) Nutch server on a user defined port
webapp          run a local Nutch web application
junit           runs the given JUnit test
or
CLASSNAME       run the class named CLASSNAME
```

Most commands print help when invoked without parameters.

After running the preceding command successfully, let's go ahead and set Apache Nutch to crawl a website. To crawl a website, we'll follow these steps:

1. Go to `%NUTCH_HOME%/conf` and edit `nutch-site.xml`. We'll add a custom configuration that will contain a custom property with a name element which contain the text `http.agent.name` and a value element which contains `SolrIndexingBookCrawler`:

    ```
    <?xml version="1.0"?>
    <?xml-stylesheet type="text/xsl" href="configuration.xsl"?>
    <configuration>
        <configuration>
          <property>
            <name>http.agent.name</name>
              <value>SolrIndexingBookCrawler</value>
          </property>
        </configuration>
    </configuration>
    ```

2. We'll create a directory to hold the list of URLs to crawl. To create this directory, we'll go to `%NUTCH_HOME%/` and execute the following command:

    ```
    $ mkdir urls
    ```

3. After creating the directory, let's create a file called `seed.txt`. This file will store the list of URLs that will be used by Apache Nutch to crawl. It will contain the following:

    ```
    http://nutch.apache.org/
    ```

4. After creating `seed.txt`, let's edit `regex-urlfilter.txt`, which is located in the `%NUTCH_HOME%/conf` folder. This regex will be used by Apache Nutch to filter the URLs that are going to be crawled. For this example, we're only going to crawl the URLs that match the following regex:

    ```
    +^http://([a-z0-9]*\.)*nutch.apache.org/
    ```

    Consider this line in `regex-urlfilter.txt`:

    ```
    # accept anything else
    +.
    ```

    Replace it with the following line:

    ```
    +^http://([a-z0-9]*\.)*nutch.apache.org/
    ```

After we have made the changes to `regex-urlfilter.txt`, let's see how we can integrate Solr with Nutch.

Configuring Solr with Nutch

Apache Solr can easily be configured for use with Nutch. We can perform the following steps to integrate Apache Nutch with Solr:

1. Create a new core (`nutch-example`) in Solr by copying the `nutch-example` folder from the `Chapter 7` code that comes with this book.

2. After creating the new core, we just need to restart the Solr instance.

3. After we have restarted the Solr instance, let's crawl some data using Nutch and index it into Solr. To do this, we'll navigate to the `%NUTCH_HOME%` folder and execute the following command:

    ```
    $ bin/crawl
    ```

    After executing the command, we'll see the following output:

    ```
    Usage: crawl [-i|--index] [-D "key=value"] <Seed Dir> <Crawl Dir>
    <Num Rounds>
            -i|--index        Indexes crawl results into a configured
    indexer
            -D                A Java property to pass to Nutch calls
            Seed Dir          Directory in which to look for a seeds
    file
            Crawl Dir         Directory where the crawl/link/segments
    dirs are saved
            Num Rounds        The number of rounds to run this crawl for
    ```

The preceding command shows us the syntax for the `crawl` command, which we're going to use for our next example. The `crawl` script is used to simplify the process involved in crawling data with Apache Nutch. It chains a number of events, which on the other hand have to be executed manually in a sequence.

To keep things simple, we'll use the following command:

```
$ bin/crawl urls crawl/ 1
```

We've used these parameters with the `crawl` script:

*   `urls`: This is the directory that contains `seed.txt` (the list of URLs to crawl)
*   `crawl`: This is the directory in which Apache Nutch stores the metadata which it receives after crawling the webpages.
*   `numOfRounds`: We're using only one round to run this crawler for this specific example

After executing the crawl command, we expect Apache Nutch to run a sequence of nutch commands that will fetch the data from the given URL (seed.txt) as per the given regex.

We'll see the following output:

```
Injecting seed URLs
/cygdrive/c/apache-nutch-1.10/bin/nutch inject crawl//crawldb urls
Injector: starting at 2015-09-10 00:11:10
Injector: crawlDb: crawl/crawldb
Injector: urlDir: urls
Injector: Converting injected urls to crawl db entries.
...
...
```

After executing the crawl command, we can index the crawl data into Solr using the following command:

```
$ bin/nutch solrindex http://localhost:8983/solr/nutch-example crawl/
crawldb/ crawl/segments/*
```

You will get the following output:

After you have executed this command, Apache Nutch will index the crawl data into Solr. The indexed data in Solr can be seen by going to the Solr Admin UI and then going to the `nutch-example` core.

Next, we can navigate to the query browser and perform a search using the (*:*) query, which will return all indexed documents. The following screenshot shows us the index URLs that are crawled by Apache Nutch and are indexed into Solr:

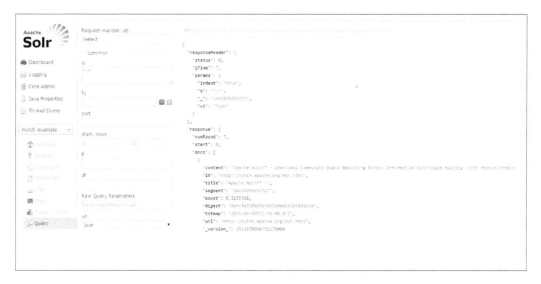

Now let's perform a `search` operation on the indexed data. Let's search for a string within the content tag of the indexed data.

We can see a JSON response after navigating to the following URL, which will search for the `Amsterdam` string in the content field:

```
http://localhost:8983/solr/nutch-example/select?q=content%3AAmsterdam
&wt=json&indent=true
```

After we have executed the query, Solr will search the indexed content field and return the result that contains the word `Amsterdam` in it.

We expect Solr to return a similar JSON response that will contain the string that was searched for with the `select` query:

```
{
responseHeader: {
status: 0,
QTime: 1,
params: {
indent: "true",
```

```
q: "content:Amsterdam",
wt: "json"
}
},
response: {
numFound: 2,
start: 0,
docs: [
{
content: "Apache Nutch™ - Downloads Community Board ......",
id: "http://nutch.apache.org/",
title: "Apache Nutch™ -",
segment: "20150910001249",
boost: 1.1978241,
digest: "f3e7a25e138b701c64bfda898b4f82f9",
tstamp: "2015-09-09T23:13:03.082Z",
url: "http://nutch.apache.org/",
_version_: 1511879509276622800
},
{
content: "Apache Nutch™ - Downloads Community Board ......",
id: "http://nutch.apache.org/index.html",
title: "Apache Nutch™ -",
segment: "20150909233727",
boost: 0.3172186,
digest: "f3e7a25e138b701c64bfda898b4f82f9",
tstamp: "2015-09-09T22:37:49.811Z",
url: "http://nutch.apache.org/index.html",
_version_: 1511878007359275000
}
]
}
}
```

As we've seen how we can use the /bin/nutch command to index data in Solr, we can also use the cleanup functionality, which is available within nutch, to keep a fresh record of the indexed data in Solr. We can remove **404 (Page not found)** links that are within Solr by executing the following command:

```
$ bin/nutch solrclean crawl/crawldb/ http://localhost:8983/solr/nutch-example
```

Thus, we've seen so far how we can easily create a simple search engine by combining Apache Nutch and Apache Solr.

There are quite a lot of configurations that we can use to optimize/tweak Apache Nutch, but that's beyond the scope of this book. You can find more information on optimization and tweaking on the Apache Nutch Wiki (`http://wiki.apache.org/nutch/`).

Summary

In this chapter, we saw how we can use Apache Nutch with Solr and combine them to create a simple search engine that will crawl the website. We also indexed the crawl data that we obtained from Nutch into Solr using the commands provided by Apache Nutch.

In the next chapter, we'll see how we can use index data in real time using the inbuilt features of Solr.

8
Commits, Real-Time Index Optimizations, and Atomic Updates

In the previous chapter, we saw how we can use Apache Nutch to crawl websites and index them in Solr. In this chapter, we'll see how we can index data in real-time using the features available from Solr 4. By using these features, the indexed data will be available in real-time for the user to see.

This chapter will cover the following topics:

- Understanding soft commit, optimize, and hard commit
- Using atomic updates to update fields
- Using RealTime Get

Understanding soft commit, optimize, and hard commit

Solr provides us a **Near-Real-Time (NRT)** search, which makes documents available for searching just after they have been indexed in Solr. Additions or updates to documents are seen nearly in real-time after we index them in Solr. This near-real-time search can be done by using a soft commit (available in Solr 4.0+), which avoids the high cost of calling fsync, and it will flush the index data into a stable storage so that it can be retrieved in the event of a JVM crash.

An optimize, on the other hand, will cause all index segments to be merged into a single segment first and then reindex them. It's just like the defragmentation that we do on an HDD, which reindexes and frees up space. Normally, index segments are merged over time as specified in the merge policy, but this happens immediately when forced using the optimize command.

Let's see how we can use soft commit and optimize in Solr. We'll use our `musicCatalog` example and create a new core based on it. We'll call our new core `musicCatalog` commit, which will contain the updated `solrconfig.xml`. The code for this core can be found in the `Chapter 8` code that comes with this book.

Let's index into Solr an XML file (`sampleAlbumData.xml`) that is available in the `Chapter 8` code examples provided with this book. We'll use the following command to do a soft commit in Solr and check out how it will be readily available for us to see from the Solr query browser.

Let's run the following command:

```
$ cd %BOOK_EXAMPLES%/Chapter-8/example-files

$ curl http://localhost:8983/solr/musicCatalog-commit/
update?softCommit=true -H "Content-Type: text/xml" --data-binary @
sampleAlbumData.xml

<?xml version="1.0" encoding="UTF-8"?>

<response>

<lst name="responseHeader"><int name="status">0</int><int
name="QTime">44</int></lst>

</response>
```

Now let's index two more files into Solr:

```
$ curl http://localhost:8983/solr/musicCatalog-commit/
update?softCommit=true -H "Content-Type: text/xml" --data-binary @
sampleAlbumData2.xml


$ curl http://localhost:8983/solr/musicCatalog-commit/
update?softCommit=true -H "Content-Type: text/xml" --data-binary @
sampleAlbumData3.xml
```

After executing this command, we can navigate to the Solr query browser by going to `http://localhost:8983/solr/#/musicCatalog-commit/query`, where we can see the index data. At this time, `softCommit` has just made the index data available for view, but there is not 100% reliability that the index data is committed into the persistence storage.

In Solr, we can also configure `softCommit` using the `autoSoftCommit` element in `solrconfig.xml`.

In `solrconfig.xml`, we'll add the following configuration:

```
<updateHandler class="solr.DirectUpdateHandler2">
    <updateLog class="solr.FSUpdateLog">
      <str name="dir">${solr.ulog.dir:}</str>
    </updateLog>

    <autoSoftCommit>
      <maxTime>10000</maxTime>
    </autoSoftCommit>
  </updateHandler>
```

The `autoSoftCommit` element accepts the following config elements:

- `maxTime`: The amount of time to wait before indexing the documents (in milliseconds)
- `maxDocs`: The number of documents to queue before indexing them in Solr

In the preceding example, `maxTime` is set to `10 seconds`, which tells Solr to perform a soft commit after 10 seconds. To test this, we can easily change `maxTime` to a higher value and then use the `curl` command to send the document to Solr. We'll see that the document won't be available in the Solr query browser until `maxTime` has elapsed.

Now we'll see how we can configure the `autoCommit` feature, which is available in `solr.DirectUpdateHandler2`. Here is an example of `autoCommit` that is available in Solr:

```
<autoCommit>
  <!-- maximum number of documents before an autocommit is
    triggered -->
  <maxDocs>2</maxDocs>

  <!-- maximum time (in MS) after adding a doc before an
    autocommit is triggered -->
  <maxTime>15000</maxTime>

  <openSearcher>false</openSearcher>
</autoCommit>
```

For more information on using `autoCommit`, visit `http://wiki.apache.org/solr/UpdateXmlMessages#A.22commit.22_and_.22optimize.22`.

Now let's see how we can update specific fields of an indexed document using atomic updates in Solr.

Using atomic updates in Solr

Atomic updates in Solr support the following sets of modifiers:

- `set`: This modifier sets or replaces a particular indexed field value
- `add`: This modifier inserts an additional value into the multi-valued fields
- `inc`: This modifier increments a numeric value

Let's see how we can update our index documents using atomic updates. To do this, we'll use the `musicCatalog` commit core that we've created in this chapter.

Let's index a new music album with some wrong values, which we will later update using the atomic update feature:

```
$ curl http://localhost:8983/solr/musicCatalog-commit/update -H "Content-Type: text/xml" --data-binary @sampleAlbumData4.xml

<?xml version="1.0" encoding="UTF-8"?>

<response>

<lst name="responseHeader"><int name="status">0</int><int name="QTime">134</int></lst>

</response>
```

We can navigate to the Solr query browser and search for the indexed data. The following figure shows the indexed data data which we've done by running the preceding command:

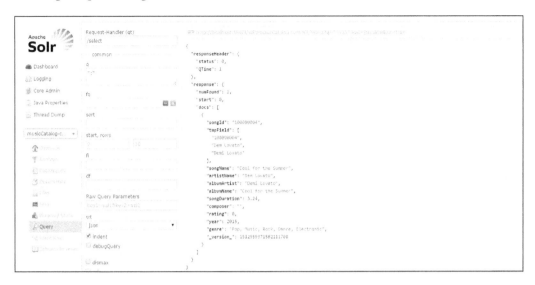

After indexing the music album, let's update its field values by sending individual update fields. Previously, we indexed an entire document that contained all the fields populated. So, to make updates, we have to create the following document, which we'll be sending to Solr:

```
<add>
  <doc>
    <field name="songId">100000004</field>
    <field name="artistName" update="set">Demi Lovato</field>
    <field name="albumName" update="set">Cool for the Summer -
      Single</field>
  </doc>
</add>
```

Let's send this to Solr to update `songId` with the value `100000004`. To do so, we'll use this command:

```
$ curl http://localhost:8983/solr/musicCatalog-commit/update -H "Content-
Type: text/xml" --data-binary @sampleAlbumData4-update.xml
```

After executing this command, we'll receive the following response from the Solr instance:

```xml
<?xml version="1.0" encoding="UTF-8"?>
<response>
<lst name="responseHeader"><int name="status">0</int><int
name="QTime">8</int></lst>
</response>
```

After we send the document, we can again use the query browser to see whether the fields have been updated or not. The following screenshot shows the query browser window:

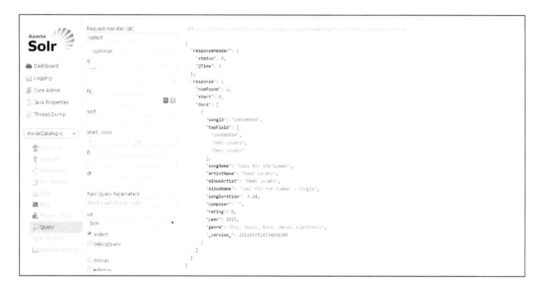

As we can see from the preceding screenshot, the `albumName` and `artistName` fields have been updated as per the XML document we sent to Solr.

Now let's see how we can use the `inc` modifier to update the rating field. We'll send this XML to update the rating field:

```xml
<add>
  <doc>
    <field name="songId">100000004</field>
    <field name="rating" update="inc">4</field>
  </doc>
</add>
```

Then we'll use the following command to send the XML to Solr to update the rating field:

```
$ curl http://localhost:8983/solr/musicCatalog-commit/update -H
"Content-Type: text/xml" --data-binary @sampleAlbumData4-update2.xml
```

```
<?xml version="1.0" encoding="UTF-8"?>
```

```
<response>
```

```
<lst name="responseHeader"><int name="status">0</int><int
name="QTime">28</int></lst>
```

```
</response>
```

We can see the updated field value after using the Solr query browser. This has shown us how we can use the update modifier to perform atomic updates in Solr, which help us update specific fields of a document rather than sending the entire document again for indexing.

Using RealTime Get

Solr also provides us with a way to see documents that are sent to it for indexing but are not indexed or have a commit/soft commit time in the future. This feature also makes Solr behave like a NoSQL data store, wherein we can fetch a document by unique key.

Let's see how we can use this feature in Solr by performing the following steps:

1. Let's add the `RealTime Get` (`/get`) request handler to `solr-config.xml`, as follows:

    ```
    <requestHandler name="/get"
      class="solr.RealTimeGetHandler">
      <lst name="defaults">
        <str name="omitHeader">true</str>
        <str name="wt">json</str>
        <str name="indent">true</str>
      </lst>
    </requestHandler>
    ```

2. After adding `requestHandler`, we'll need to change `updateLog` in `updateHandler`. This is because `RealTime Get` uses the `updateLog` feature to work. The `updateLog` element or transaction log is a feature in Solr wherein data is written to a transaction log file before indexing. During startup, the transaction log file is read, so in the event of a failure, there won't be any data loss. More information can be found at `https://cwiki.apache.org/confluence/display/solr/RealTime+Get`:

```
<updateLog class="solr.FSUpdateLog">
    <str name="dir">${solr.data.dir:}</str>
</updateLog>
```

3. Once we have updated the `updateLog` element, we'll restart our Solr instance. After restarting our Solr instance, let's send some JSON data with a `commitWithin` parameter in the URL. The `commitWithin` parameter will tell Solr to wait for a specific duration of time before indexing the document in Solr:

```
$ curl http://localhost:8983/solr/musicCatalog-commit/
update?commitWithin=10000000 -H "Content-type:application/json"
--data-binary @sampleAlbum5.json
```

This will result in the following response from the Solr instance:

```
{"responseHeader":{"status":0,"QTime":41}}
```

4. When we navigate to the Solr query browser, we see that the document is not returning with the Solr query browser, as it's not indexed until the `commitWithin` element time lapses: `http://localhost:8983/solr/musicCatalog-commit/select?q=songId:100000008`

We'll get the following response from the Solr instance:

```
<response>
  <lst name="responseHeader">
    <int name="status">0</int>
    <int name="QTime">1</int>
  </lst>
  <result name="response" numFound="0" start="0"/>
</response>
```

As there is no index document with songId: 100000008, Solr will not return any documents.

5. At this point, we can use the `RealTime Get` handler to retrieve the document. We can use the following command to retrieve the document that was sent to Solr for indexing: `http://localhost:8983/solr/musicCatalog-commit/get?id=100000008`

After running this command in the browser, we'll see the document that was sent to Solr for indexing:

```
{
doc: {
songId: "100000008",
songName: "Drag Me Down",
artistName: "One Direction",
albumArtist: "",
albumName: "Drag Me Down - Single",
songDuration: 3.12,
composer: "",
rating: 0,
year: 2015,
genre: "Pop, Music, Rock",
_version_: 1512962668868141000
}
}
```

This shows us how we can use `RealTime Get` to use, for example, a NoSQL data store. In it, we can use the `/get` request handler to get documents that were sent for indexing, even if they are not indexed in Solr.

Summary

In this chapter, we saw how we can perform atomic updates, soft commit, and optimize in Solr, which will help us to get indexed data faster and also to perform field updates on indexed documents. Then we saw how we can use new features in Solr (4.0 onwards) to get better search results based on real-time indexing data.

In the next chapter, we will cover advanced topics such as multilanguage indexing, deduplication, and UIMA support in Solr.

9
Advanced Topics – Multilanguage, Deduplication, and Others

In the previous chapter, we saw how we can use Solr to retrieve documents that are indexed into it in real time. In this chapter, we'll cover some advanced topics that will help us use the full potential of Solr.

Specifically, we'll cover the following topics in this chapter:

- Indexing a document in multiple languages
- Detecting duplicate documents (deduplication)
- Streaming of documents in Solr (content streaming)
- UIMA integration with Solr

Multilanguage indexing

Solr provides us with a way to index multilanguage documents in it. In this section, we'll cover how to easily index multilanguage documents in Solr and also how to auto-detect a document language.

Let's create a new core called languages-example. It will contain the following fields in schema.xml, which we're going to use for our example:

```
<fields>
  <field name="id" type="string" indexed="true" stored="true"
  required="true"/>
```

```
        <field name="content" type="text_general" indexed="true"
        stored="true" />
        <field name="text" type="text_general" multiValued="true"
        indexed="true" stored="false" />
        <copyField source="content" dest="text" />
        <field name="language" type="string" stored="true"
        indexed="true" />

        <dynamicField name="*_en" type="text_en" stored="true"
        indexed="true" />
        <dynamicField name="*_ru" type="text_ru" stored="true"
        indexed="true" />
        <dynamicField name="*_fr" type="text_fr" stored="true"
        indexed="true" />
    </fields>
```

After we have added the fields, we'll modify our `solrconfig.xml` configuration file to add the language detection feature, which is provided by LangDetect (`http://code.google.com/p/language-detection/`):

```
    <lib dir="${user.dir}/../contrib/analysis-extras/lucene-libs/" />
    <lib dir="${user.dir}/../contrib/analysis-extras/lib/" />
    <lib dir="${user.dir}/../dist/" regex="solr-langid-.*\.jar" />
    <lib dir="${user.dir}/../contrib/langid/lib/" />
```

Next, after adding the libraries, we'll add an `UpdateRequestProcessorChain` element, which will contain the language detection processor:

```
    <updateRequestProcessorChain name="languages">
      <processor
      class="solr.LangDetectLanguageIdentifierUpdateProcessorFactory">
      <lst name="invariants">
        <str name="langid.fl">content</str>
        <str name="langid.whitelist">en,fr,ru</str>
        <str name="langid.fallback">en</str>
        <str name="langid.langField">language</str>
        <bool name="langid.map">true</bool>
        <bool name="langid.map.keepOrig">false</bool>
      </lst>
      </processor>
    <processor class="solr.RunUpdateProcessorFactory" />
    </updateRequestProcessorChain>
```

We've added the `solr.LangDetectLanguageIdentifierUpdateProcessorFactory` class in `UpdateRequestProcessor`, which will automatically detect the language from the document and will store it in the `language` field.

Alternatively, we can use `solr.TikaLanguageIdentifierUpdateProcessorFactory` to detect the language of the document.

 More information on using the processor factory is available at `https://cwiki.apache.org/confluence/display/solr/Detecting+Languages+During+Indexing`.

We'll be indexing the following XML file (`multilang-doc.xml`), which will contain three separate documents in English, Russian, and French:

```
<add>
  <!-- English -->
  <doc>
    <field name="id">doc1</field>
    <field name="content">
      <![CDATA[Hello, This is an example for the Solr Indexing
      book.]]>
    </field>
  </doc>

  <!-- Russian -->
  <doc>
    <field name="id">doc2</field>
    <field name="content">
      <![CDATA[▨▨▨▨▨ , ▨▨▨ ▨▨▨▨▨ ▨▨▨ ▨▨▨▨▨▨▨▨▨ ▨▨▨▨▨ Solr.]]>
    </field>
  </doc>

  <!-- French -->
  <doc>
    <field name="id">doc3</field>
    <field name="content">
      <![CDATA[Bonjour, Ceci est un exemple pour le livre
      d'indexation Solr.]]>
    </field>
  </doc>

</add>
```

Let's go ahead and index the document in our newly created core. To do this, we'll start up Solr and run the following command:

```
$ curl 'http://localhost:8983/solr/languages-
example/update?commit=true' -H "Content-Type: text/xml" --data-binary
@multilang-doc.xml
```

After we execute the command, we'll see the following output from Solr, which confirms that it has been successful in sending the document to Solr:

```
<?xml version="1.0" encoding="UTF-8"?>
<response>
<lst name="responseHeader"><int name="status">0</int><int
name="QTime">513</int></lst>
</response>
```

After indexing, let's go ahead and query the indexed data in Solr. So, open up the Solr Query browser or go to `http://localhost:8983/solr/languages-example/select?q=*%3A*&wt=json&indent=true`.

We can see the following response from the server:

```
{
  responseHeader : {
    status : 0,
    QTime : 2
  },
  response : {
    numFound : 3,
    start : 0,
    docs : [{
      id : "doc1",
      language : "en",
      content_en : " Hello, This is an example for the Solr
      Indexing book. "
    }, {
      id : "doc2",
      language : "ru",
      content_ru : " ▨▨▨▨▨ , ▨▨▨ ▨▨▨▨▨ ▨▨▨ ▨▨▨▨▨▨▨▨▨ ▨▨▨▨▨
      Solr. "
    }, {
      id : "doc3",
      language : "fr",
      content_fr : " Bonjour, Ceci est un exemple pour le livre
      d'indexation Solr. "
    }
    ]
  }
}
```

As we can see from the preceding response – the language field has been auto-populated by `solr.LangDetectLanguageIdentifierUpdateProcessorFactory` – we can realize how easy it is to index multilanguage documents in Solr.

We can also create separate search handlers based on the language. An example of using various language handlers has been provided in `solrconfig.xml`, which is available in the code examples.

The following is an example of a sample search handler (`/selectRU`) that we can use to search for documents whose language is set to Russian (`ru`):

```
<requestHandler name="/selectRU" class="solr.SearchHandler" >
  <lst name="invariants">
    <str name="fq">language:ru</str>
  </lst>
</requestHandler>
```

In the Solr Query browser, we can search for all documents whose language is Russian using the `/selectRU` search handler. Here is a screenshot that shows the use of this handler:

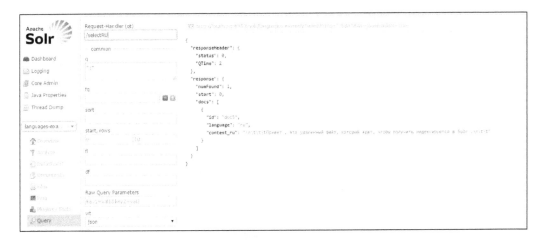

Now let's move on to a different topic, which will help us remove duplicate documents from our index. In the next section, we'll see how we can use `SignatureUpdateProcessorFactory` to remove/overwrite duplicate elements.

Removing duplicate documents (deduplication)

Solr provides us with a way to prevent duplicate or nearly duplicate elements to get indexed using a signature/fingerprint field. It natively provides a deduplication technique of this type via the signature class, and this can further be used to implement new hash and signature implementations.

Let's see how we can implement deduplication in Solr. We'll use our `musicCatalog` core, which we used in the previous chapter as well, and will modify it:

1. Copy the `musicCatalog` core and create a new core called `musicCatalog-dedupe` from it. After we have created the new core, we'll change `schema.xml` to add a signature field that will contain the document signature/fingerprint:

```
<!-- Field to store the fingerprint/signature -->
<field name="signature" type="string" indexed="true" stored="true"
required="true" multiValued="false" />
```

2. After adding the field, we'll add a new `UpdateRequestProcessor` element to `solrconfig.xml` configuration file, which will detect and overwrite duplicate documents:

```
<updateRequestProcessorChain name="dedupe">
  <processor class="org.apache.solr.update.processor
  .SignatureUpdateProcessorFactory">
    <bool name="enabled">true</bool>
    <bool name="overwriteDupes">true</bool>
    <str name="signatureField">signature</str>
    <str
    name="fields">songId,songName,artistName,albumArtist,
    albumName,songDuration,composer,rating,year,genre</str>
    <str name="signatureClass">org.apache.solr.update
    .processor.TextProfileSignature</str>
  </processor>
  <processor class="solr.LogUpdateProcessorFactory" />
  <processor class="solr.RunUpdateProcessorFactory" />
</updateRequestProcessorChain>
```

We've used the `SignatureUpdateProcessorFactory` class that comes with Solr, which we can use to detect/overwrite duplicate documents. The following properties can be set up in `SignatureUpdateProcessorFactory`:

- `signatureClass`: This is an implementation of the `org.apache.solr.update.processor.Signature` abstract class, for example, `org.apache.solr.update.processor.Lookup3Signature` or `solr.processor.Lookup3Signature`.

- `fields`: These are the names of the fields that are used to generate the hash. By default, all fields of the document will be used to generate the hash.

- `signatureField`: This is the name of the field that will hold the hash. This should be defined in `schema.xml`.

- ○ enabled: This is used to enable/disable deduplication.
- ○ overwriteDupes: If this is set to true, the matching document will be overwritten.

3. After we add the UpdateRequestHandler, we'll use the following XML document (duplicateAlbumData.xml), which contains two duplicate documents, and will send it to Solr for indexing:

```xml
<add>
  <doc>
    <field name="songId">100000001</field>
    <field name="songName">Cool for the Summer</field>
    <field name="artistName">Dem Lovato</field>
    <field name="albumArtist">Demi Lovato</field>
    <field name="albumName">Cool for the Summer</field>
    <field name="songDuration">3.24</field>
    <field name="composer"/>
    <field name="rating">3.5</field>
    <field name="year">2015</field>
    <field name="genre">Pop, Music, Rock, Dance,
    Electronic</field>
  </doc>
  <doc>
    <field name="songId">100000001</field>
    <field name="songName">Cool for the Summer</field>
    <field name="artistName">Dem Lovato</field>
    <field name="albumArtist">Demi Lovato</field>
    <field name="albumName">Cool for the Summer</field>
    <field name="songDuration">3.24</field>
    <field name="composer"/>
    <field name="rating">3.5</field>
    <field name="year">2015</field>
    <field name="genre">Pop, Music, Rock, Dance,
    Electronic</field>
  </doc>
</add>
```

We can use the following command to send the XML file that contains these two duplicate documents for indexing:

```
$ curl 'http://localhost:8983/solr/musicCatalog-dedupe/update?update.
chain=dedupe&commit=true' -H "Content-Type: text/xml" --data-binary @
duplicateAlbumData.xml
```

After executing this command, we'll get the following response from Solr:

```
<?xml version="1.0" encoding="UTF-8"?>
<response>
<lst name="responseHeader"><int name="status">0</int><int
name="QTime">383</int></lst>
</response>
```

After we execute this query, we can use the `q=*:*` query to view the data that was indexed into Solr.

Open up the Solr Query browser or using the following url `http://localhost:8983/solr/musicCatalog-dedupe/select?q=*%3A*&wt=json&indent=true`.

We'll receive the following response from Solr:

```
{
  responseHeader : {
  status : 0,
  QTime : 3
  },
  response : {
    numFound : 1,
    start : 0,
    docs : [{
      songId : "100000001",
      songName : "Cool for the Summer",
      artistName : "Dem Lovato",
      albumArtist : "Demi Lovato",
      albumName : "Cool for the Summer",
      songDuration : 3.24,
      composer : "",
      rating : 3.5,
      year : 2015,
      genre : "Pop, Music, Rock, Dance, Electronic",
      signature : "c105d2c9b431932e0e662b513f328aaa"
    }
    ]
  }
}
```

As we can see from this response, the original document has been overwritten and we're seeing only one document getting indexed in Solr.

Content streaming

In Solr, we can index remote or local files by enabling remote streaming in
`solrconfig.xml`. Let's see how we can use this feature in Solr, we'll follow
the steps given here to enable the remote streaming feature.

Let's use our newly created `languages-example` core and modify `solrconfig.xml`.
We'll replace the `requestDispatcher` config in our `solrconfig.xml` file with the
following lines:

```
<requestDispatcher handleSelect="false" >
  <requestParsers enableRemoteStreaming="true"
    multipartUploadLimitInKB="2048000"
    formdataUploadLimitInKB="2048"
    addHttpRequestToContext="false"/>
</requestDispatcher>
```

The `enableRemoteStreaming="true"` property will enable the remote streaming
feature. This will enable us to index remote or local files. Let's go ahead and index
a remote file in our Solr index:

```
$ curl http://localhost:8983/solr/languages-
example/update?commit=true -F
stream.url=https://raw.githubusercontent.com/sachin-
handiekar/SolrIndexingBook/master/Chapter-9/files/multilang-
remote.xml
```

We'll get the following response from Solr:

```
<?xml version="1.0" encoding="UTF-8"?>
<response>
<lst name="responseHeader"><int name="status">0</int><int
name="QTime">968</int></lst>
</response>
```

We can see the indexed document in Solr after navigating to the query browser.
We'll get this output:

```
{
  responseHeader : {
    status : 0,
    QTime : 8
  },
  response : {
    numFound : 3,
    start : 0,
    docs : [{
```

```
      id : "doc4",
      language : "en",
      content_en : " Hello, This is a remote file which is waiting
      to get indexed in Solr. "
  }, {
      id : "doc5",
      language : "ru",
      content_ru : " ▨▨▨▨▨ , ▨▨▨ ▨▨▨▨▨▨▨▨ ▨▨▨▨, ▨▨▨▨▨▨ ▨▨▨▨,
      ▨▨▨▨ ▨▨▨▨▨▨▨ ▨▨▨▨▨▨▨▨▨▨▨▨ ▨ Solr . "
  }, {
      id : "doc6",
      language : "fr",
      content_fr : " Bonjour, ceci est un fichier distant qui est
      en attente pour obtenir indexé dans Solr. "
  }
  ]
}
}
```

As we can see from the preceding response, the original document has been overwritten and we're just seeing one document getting indexed in Solr.

We can also use `DumpRequestHandler` to debug the requests that are made by adding the following request handler in `solrconfig.xml`:

```
<requestHandler name="/debug/dump" class="solr.DumpRequestHandler"
/>
```

For example, let's see the contents of the remote file that we recently indexed into Solr. When we navigate to the following URL, we'll see the XML response from the `/debug/dump` request handler; it will contain the stream response:

```
http://localhost:8983/solr/languages-example/debug/dump?stream.
url=https://raw.githubusercontent.com/sachin-handiekar/
SolrIndexingBook/master/Chapter-9/files/multilang-remote.xml
```

This URL will return the following XML response, which will contain the data of the remote file:

```
▼<response>
  ▼<lst name="responseHeader">
     <int name="status">0</int>
     <int name="QTime">389</int>
   </lst>
  ▼<lst name="params">
   ▼<str name="stream.url">
       https://raw.githubusercontent.com/sachin-handiekar/SolrIndexingBook/master/Chapter-9/files/multilang-remote.xml
     </str>
   </lst>
  ▼<arr name="streams">
   ▼<lst>
       <null name="name"/>
       <str name="sourceInfo">url</str>
       <null name="size"/>
       <null name="contentType"/>
     ▼<str name="stream">
         <?xml version="1.0" encoding="UTF-8" ?> <add> <!-- English --> <doc> <field name="id">doc4</field> <field name="content"> <![CDATA[Hello, This is a
         remote file which is waiting to get indexed in Solr.]]> </field> </doc> <!-- Russian --> <doc> <field name="id">doc5</field> <field name="content">
         <![CDATA[Привет , это удаленный файл, который ждет, чтобы получить индексируются в Solr .]]> </field> </doc> <!-- French --> <doc> <field
         name="id">doc6</field> <field name="content"> <![CDATA[Bonjour, ceci est un fichier distant qui est en attente pour obtenir indexé dans Solr.]]>
         </field> </doc> </add>
       </str>
     </lst>
   </arr>
  ▼<lst name="context">
     <str name="webapp">/solr</str>
     <str name="path">/debug/dump</str>
   </lst>
 </response>
```

The use of the `/debug/dump` request handler should be disabled in production, as anyone can see the contents of the remote/local file, which creates a security risk.

UIMA integration with Solr

Solr can also be integrated with Apache **UIMA** (short for **Unstructured Information Management Architecture**), which can be used to define a custom pipeline to add metadata to documents.

 More information about Solr UIMA integration can be found at `https://wiki.apache.org/solr/SolrUIMA`.

In Solr, UIMA can be configured by following these steps:

1. In `solrconfig.xml`, we can add the following libraries:

   ```
   <lib dir="../../contrib/uima/lib" />
   <lib dir="../../dist/" regex="solr-uima-\d.*\.jar" />
   ```

2. After adding the libraries, we can add the following fields to `schema.xml`, which will contain the language, concept, and sentence fields:

   ```
   <field name="language" type="string" indexed="true"
   stored="true" required="false"/>
   <field name="concept" type="string" indexed="true"
   stored="true" multiValued="true" required="false"/>
   ```

```
<field name="sentence" type="text" indexed="true"
stored="true" multiValued="true" required="false" />
```

3. After adding these fields, we'll add the `org.apache.solr.uima.
processor.UIMAUpdateRequestProcessorFactory` class to
`UpdateRequestProcessorChain`, which will contain the connection details
and more configuration-related settings for UIMA:

```
<updateRequestProcessorChain name="uima">
  <processor class="org.apache.solr.uima.processor
  .UIMAUpdateRequestProcessorFactory">
    <lst name="uimaConfig">
    <lst name="runtimeParameters">
      <str name="keyword_apikey">VALID_ALCHEMYAPI_KEY</str>
      <str name="concept_apikey">VALID_ALCHEMYAPI_KEY</str>
      <str name="lang_apikey">VALID_ALCHEMYAPI_KEY</str>
        <str name="cat_apikey">VALID_ALCHEMYAPI_KEY</str>
        <str
        name="entities_apikey">VALID_ALCHEMYAPI_KEY</str>
        <str name="oc_licenseID">VALID_OPENCALAIS_KEY</str>
    </lst>
    <str name="analysisEngine">/org/apache/uima/desc
    /OverridingParamsExtServicesAE.xml</str>
    <!-- Set to true if you want to continue indexing
    even if text processing fails.
    Default is false. That is, Solr throws
    RuntimeException and
    never indexed documents entirely in your session. -->
    <bool name="ignoreErrors">true</bool>
    <!-- This is optional. It is used for logging when
    text processing fails.
    If logField is not specified, uniqueKey will be used
    as logField.
    <str name="logField">id</str>
    -->
    <lst name="analyzeFields">
      <bool name="merge">false</bool>
      <arr name="fields">
        <str>text</str>
      </arr>
    </lst>
    <lst name="fieldMappings">
      <lst name="type">
        <str
        name="name">org.apache.uima.alchemy.ts.concept
        .ConceptFS</str>
```

```
      <lst name="mapping">
        <str name="feature">text</str>
        <str name="field">concept</str>
      </lst>
    </lst>
    <lst name="type">
      <str name="name">org.apache.uima.alchemy.ts
      .language.LanguageFS</str>
      <lst name="mapping">
        <str name="feature">language</str>
        <str name="field">language</str>
      </lst>
    </lst>
    <lst name="type">
      <str name="name">org.apache.uima
      .SentenceAnnotation</str>
      <lst name="mapping">
        <str name="feature">coveredText</str>
        <str name="field">sentence</str>
      </lst>
    </lst>
      </lst>
    </lst>
  </processor>
  <processor class="solr.LogUpdateProcessorFactory" />
  <processor class="solr.RunUpdateProcessorFactory" />
</updateRequestProcessorChain>
```

4. Finally in `solrconfig.xml`, we'll use the following `UpdateRequestHandler`, which will contain `uima` as the default update processor:

```
<requestHandler name="/update" class="solr.
XmlUpdateRequestHandler">
  <lst name="defaults">
    <str name="update.processor">uima</str>
  </lst>
</requestHandler>
```

The preceding settings can be used to integrate Solr with UIMA, which can be used to enrich our indexed documents with metadata received from UIMA.

 More information about UIMA can be found at `http://cwiki.apache.org/confluence/display/UIMA/`.

Summary

In this chapter, we saw how Solr can be used to index multilanguage documents with some easy configuration, and also language detection, which can be used to automatically detect the language of a document. Plus, we covered the deduplication technique, which Solr supports natively. It can be used to overwrite/remove documents from Solr using the hashing/fingerprint technique. We also covered in brief content streaming and the integration of Apache UIMA with Solr.

In the next chapter, we'll cover how we can easily set up a cluster of Solr servers.

10
Distributed Indexing

In the previous chapter, we covered advanced topics in Solr, such as multilanguage support, deduplication, content streaming, and so on. In this chapter, we'll see how we can set up a cluster of Solr servers that will provide a fault-tolerant and high-availability scenario. We'll cover the following topics:

- Setting up SolrCloud
- Using the collections API
- Distributed indexing and searching

Setting up SolrCloud

In this section, we will see how we can set up multiple nodes of Solr servers on a single physical machine. We'll clone the example folder that comes with the default Solr installation to create multiple shards.

Let's go ahead and set up a two-node Solr instance. We'll navigate to our Solr instance and execute the following command:

```
$ cd $SOLR_HOME
$ cp -r example shard1
$ cp -r example shard2
```

After running the preceding commands, we'll see that there are two folders (shard1 and shard2) that are now ready.

Let's go ahead and start the two `solr` nodes that we just created. To do this, we'll navigate to `$SOLR_HOME/bin` folder:

- `shard1`:

```
$ ./solr start -cloud -d ../shard1 -p 8983
```

- `shard2`:

```
$ ./solr start -cloud -d ../shard2 -p 8987 -z localhost:9983
```

After running the two nodes, we can navigate to `http://localhost:8983/solr` and can see a **Cloud** tab activated. This example was performed on a fresh installation of Solr, so the results will be different if we don't use a fresh installation. The following screenshot shows us the Graph view of the SolrCloud:

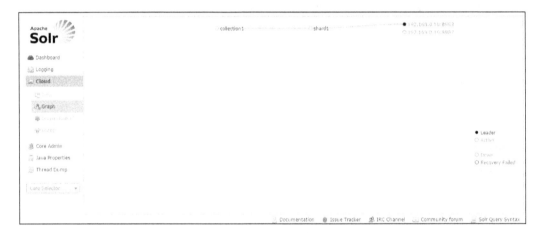

As we can see from the Solr **Cloud** tab, the default configuration contains two nodes, which contain a shard, one of them being the shard leader and the other being a replica.

Let's create a new collection using the collections API and assign to it two shards and two replicas that we can use.

But before we do this, we'll create a default configuration for the collection and upload it to `ZooKeeper`. The configuration stored in `ZooKeeper` is shared between the nodes that are running in `SolrCloud`. Any changes made in the configuration can then be made available on all the instances within the `SolrCloud` that are using that configuration:

```
$ $SOLR_HOME/example/scripts/cloud-scripts/zkcli.sh -zkhost
localhost:9983 -cmd upconfig -confdir $SOLR_HOME/example/solr/
collection1/conf -confname default
```

Note that Windows users can use the `zkcli.bat` version of the script or the following Java command:

```
$ java -classpath "example\solr-webapp\webapp\WEB-INF\
lib\*;example\lib\ext\*" org.apache.solr.cloud.ZkCLI -cmd
upconfig -zkhost localhost:9983 -confdir $SOLR_HOME/example/solr/
collection1/conf -confname default
```

After uploading the collection configuration to `ZooKeeper`, we'll create a collection named `musicCatalogue-solrcloud`:

```
curl "http://localhost:8983/solr/admin/collections?action=CREATE&name=
musicCatalogue-solrcloud&replicationFactor=2&numShards=2&collection.co
nfigName=default&maxShardsPerNode=2&wt=json&indent=2"
```

We'll get the following response from the Solr instance:

```
{
  "responseHeader":{
    "status":0,
    "QTime":8549},
  "success":{
    "":{
      "responseHeader":{
        "status":0,
        "QTime":7582},
      "core":"musicCatalogue-solrcloud_shard1_replica2"},
    "":{
      "responseHeader":{
        "status":0,
        "QTime":7641},
      "core":"musicCatalogue-solrcloud_shard2_replica2"},
    "":{
      "responseHeader":{
        "status":0,
        "QTime":7912},
      "core":"musicCatalogue-solrcloud_shard2_replica1"},
    "":{
      "responseHeader":{
        "status":0,
        "QTime":7982},
      "core":"musicCatalogue-solrcloud_shard1_replica
  }
```

After we have done this, we can navigate to the Solr **Cloud** tab. The following screenshot shows us the two different shards which were created:

Now let's just test our new collection by indexing some data in it. We'll use the following command to index the data in Solr:

```
$ curl 'http://localhost:8983/solr/musicCatalogue-solrcloud/
json?commit=true' -H 'Content-type:application/json' -d '
[
  {"id" : "1", "title" : "Apache Solr Indexing Data"},
  {"id" : "2", "title" : "Apache Solr Cookbook"}
]'
```

After running the command, we should get the following response from Solr, telling us that the documents were indexed successfully:

```
{"responseHeader":{"status":0,"QTime":237}}
```

The collections API

The collections API supports the following operations, which can be used to create, remove, or reload collections:

- CREATE: Creates a collection
- RELOAD: Reloads a collection
- SPLITSHARD: Splits a shard into two new shards
- CREATESHARD: Creates a new shard
- DELETESHARD: Deletes an inactive shard

There are more operations available, and they can be found on the Solr Wiki. In this chapter, we'll just see how we can use the collections API to manage a Solr configuration.

Let's go ahead and create a new collection with the number of shards as 2. To do this, we'll execute the following command:

```
curl "http://localhost:8983/solr/admin/collections?action=CREATE&name=sam
pleCatalog&replicationFactor=2&numShards=2&collection.configName=default&
maxShardsPerNode=2&wt=json&indent=2"
```

We'll get the output as follows after running this command:

```
{
  "responseHeader":{
    "status":0,
    "QTime":10346},
  "success":{
    "":{
      "responseHeader":{
        "status":0,
        "QTime":9381},
      "core":"sampleCatalog_shard1_replica1"},
    "":{
      "responseHeader":{
        "status":0,
        "QTime":9565},
      "core":"sampleCatalog_shard1_replica2"},
    "":{
      "responseHeader":{
        "status":0,
        "QTime":9689},
      "core":"sampleCatalog_shard2_replica1"},
    "":{
      "responseHeader":{
        "status":0,
        "QTime":9774},
      "core":"sampleCatalog_shard2_replica2"}}}
```

After creating the new catalog, we can navigate to the **Cloud** tab in Solr Admin UI. We can see that our new core has been created.

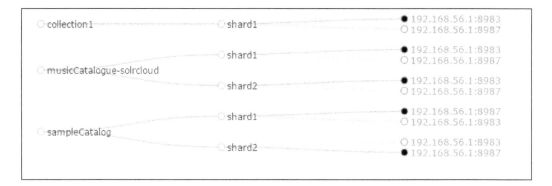

Now, let's use the collections API to delete the newly created collection. We'll use the following command to delete it:

```
curl "http://localhost:8983/solr/admin/collections?action=DELETE&name=
sampleCatalog&wt=json&indent=2"
```

We'll get this response after running the preceding command:

```
{
  "responseHeader": {
    "status": 0,
    "QTime": 1272
  },
  "success": {
    "192.168.56.1:8983_solr": {
      "responseHeader": {
        "status": 0,
        "QTime": 182
      }
    },
    "192.168.56.1:8983_solr": {
      "responseHeader": {
        "status": 0,
        "QTime": 209
      }
    },
    "192.168.56.1:8987_solr": {
      "responseHeader": {
        "status": 0,
        "QTime": 200
      }
    },
```

```
"192.168.56.1:8987_solr": {
  "responseHeader": {
    "status": 0,
    "QTime": 216
  }
}
}
}
}
```

After we have run the `delete` query, we can run the `list` command to get the current list of collections.

To do this, we use the following command:

```
curl "http://localhost:8983/solr/admin/collections?action=LIST&wt=jso
n&indent=2"
```

We'll get this response:

```
{
  "responseHeader": {
    "status": 0,
    "QTime": 283
  },
  "collections": [
    "collection1",
    "musicCatalogue-solrcloud"
  ]
}
```

We've seen how we can create and delete collections. Now let's see one more feature of the collections API. We can create an alias using this API.

Let's create an alias for our collection using this command:

```
curl "http://localhost:8983/solr/admin/collections?action=CREA
TEALIAS&name=musicCatalogue-alias&collections=musicCatalogue-
solrcloud&wt=json&indent=2"
```

After running it, we should get the following response:

```
{
  "responseHeader": {
    "status": 0,
    "QTime": 282
  }
}
```

Now, let's use the alias we've just created and run a query against it:

```
curl "http://localhost:8983/solr/musicCatalogue-alias/select?q=*%3A*&w
t=json&indent=true"
```

We'll get this response:

```
{
  "responseHeader": {
    "status": 0,
    "QTime": 32,
    "params": {
      "q": "*:*",
      "indent": "true",
      "wt": "json"
    }
  },
  "response": {
    "numFound": 3,
    "start": 0,
    "maxScore": 1.0,
    "docs": [
      {
        "id": "1",
        "title": [
          "Apache Solr Indexing Data"
        ],
        "_version_": 1516224129180631040
      },
      {
        "id": "2",
        "title": [
          "Apache Solr Cookbook"
        ],
        "_version_": 1516224138192093184
      }
    ]
  }
}
```

This shows us how we can create an alias for a collection using the Collections API. One of the main benefits of using an alias is that it hides the main collection from the search client application. For example, we can have an alias named **onlineArticles**; when queried, it can return documents from magazines and blogs collections.

An alias can also be deleted using the following command:

```
curl "http://localhost:8983/solr/admin/collections?action=DELETEALIAS&
name=musicCatalogue-alias&wt=json&indent=2"
```

> More information about the Collections API can be found at https://cwiki.apache.org/confluence/display/solr/Collections+API.

Updating configuration files

There is always a need to update configuration files in Solr. In Solr, while using SolrCloud, we can always maintain the configuration files in SVN, Git, or any other version control tool. Any changes in the configuration file can be pushed to the ZooKeeper instance that will keep all the Solr instances in sync with the latest version of the configuration.

Let's now see how we can update an instance of a file in ZooKeeper. To do this, we'll create a new file in the conf directory, which we'll then push to Zookeeper using the zkcli script.

We create a new file called updateMe.conf in %SOLR_HOME%/example/solr/collection1/conf. After this we run the following command, which will push the file:

```
$ $SOLR_HOME/example/scripts/cloud-scripts/zkcli.sh -zkhost
localhost:9983 -cmd upconfig -confdir %SOLR_HOME%/example/solr/
collection1/conf -confname default
```

After running this command, we can navigate to the **Cloud** tab and then click on the **Tree** button, which will show us the files that are available in the Zookeeper instance. We can see in the following screenshot that our newly created file is present in the /configs/default location:

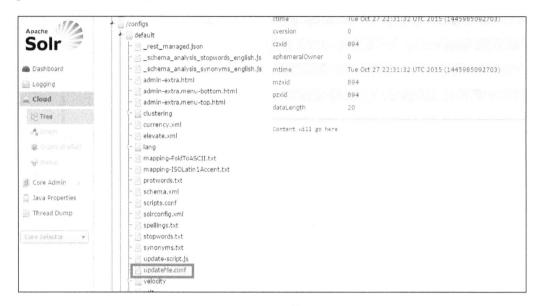

After updating the collection, we should always reload it, which will load up any changes made in the configuration files. We can reload a collection using the Collections API, like this:

```
curl "http://localhost:8983/solr/admin/collections?action=RELOAD&name=
musicCatalogue-solrcloud&wt=json&indent=2"
```

We've discussed new terms in this chapter such as **sharding** and **replication**. Let's see what these terms mean in SolrCloud:

- **Sharding**: In Solr, sharding allows us to break down a large index into multiple smaller indexes that can fit on one server and can help us parallelize complex query execution and index operations.

- **Replication**: In Solr, replicas can help us create additional copies of a Solr index across multiple servers to add redundancy/failover scenarios. Replication also helps us increase the number of queries that an index can execute concurrently.

The Solr Cloud view also shows the configuration that was sent to `ZooKeeper`. The following screenshot shows the Solr Cloud view:

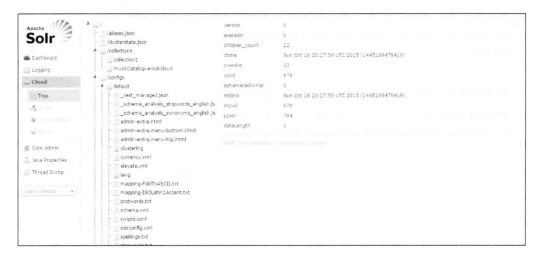

The **Cloud** tab contains the graph (radial) view, which can be used to see the shards and replicas currently being used in a graphical way. This screenshot shows our collection in a radial view:

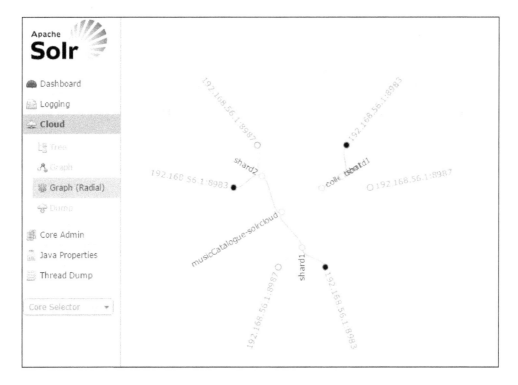

Distributed indexing and searching

In `SolrCloud`, the main goal behind distributed indexing is to send a document to any node in the cluster and have that document indexed in the shard.

Solr uses a document router to assign a document to a shard. There are two basic document routing strategies:

- `compositeId` (default)
- Implicit

In `compositeId` (default), when we send documents to Solr for indexing, Solr uses the hash of the document to distribute the load to multiple Solr instances. Previously in this chapter, we added a few documents to the index. Now let's see how Solr distributes the load to multiple Solr instances.

As we're running two instances of Solr locally (`shard1` on `8983` and `shard2` on `8987`), we'll run the following two queries with the `distrib` flag set to `false`. The flag will tell Solr to run the query in a non-distributed way, which means the result that we will get will be only for the shard on which the query is running:

- `shard1`:

  ```
  curl "http://localhost:8983/solr/musicCatalogue-solrcloud/select?q
  =*%3A*&distrib=false&rows=0&wt=json&indent=true"
  ```

- `shard2`:

  ```
  curl "http://localhost:8987/solr/musicCatalogue-solrcloud/select?q
  =*%3A*&distrib=false&rows=0&wt=json&indent=true"
  ```

After running it, we'll get this response on each of the shards:

```
{
  "responseHeader": {
    "status": 0,
    "QTime": 1,
    "params": {
      "q": "*:*",
      "distrib": "false",
      "indent": "true",
      "rows": "0",
      "wt": "json"
    }
  },
  "response": {
```

```
            "numFound": 1,
            "start": 0,
            "docs": []
        }
    }
```

As we can see from the preceding response, two documents that we've indexed previously have gone to two different instances. Now let's run the query one more time, this time with the distributed request flag set to true (default), and we return the id and shard using the fl flag:

```
curl "http://localhost:8983/solr/musicCatalogue-solrcloud/select?q=*%3
A*&wt=json&indent=true&fl=id,[shard]"
```

We'll get the following response from Solr:

```
{
    "responseHeader": {
        "status": 0,
        "QTime": 29,
        "params": {
            "q": "*:*",
            "indent": "true",
            "fl": "id,[shard]",
            "wt": "json"
        }
    },
    "response": {
        "numFound": 2,
        "start": 0,
        "maxScore": 1.0,
        "docs": [
            {
                "id": "1",
                "[shard]": "http://192.168.56.1:8983/solr/musicCatalogue-
solrcloud_shard1_replica1/|http://192.168.56.1:8987/solr/
musicCatalogue-solrcloud_shard1_replica2/"
            },
            {
                "id": "2",
                "[shard]": "http://192.168.56.1:8983/solr/musicCatalogue-
solrcloud_shard2_replica1/|http://192.168.56.1:8987/solr/
musicCatalogue-solrcloud_shard2_replica2/"
            }
        ]
    }
}
```

As we can see, both the documents have gone to two different shards, which are `musicCatalogue-solrcloud_shard1_replica2` and `musicCatalogue-solrcloud_shard2_replica2`.

We've thus seen how Solr automatically distributes documents to different Solr shards. In Solr, we can also stop this feature using the `solr.NoOpDistributingUpdateProcessorFactory` processor, which will help us send documents to just one node and not distribute the load among shards. We might have a requirement where we want to use only one of the nodes to store a specific type of document. For this specific scenario, we can use the `solr.NoOpDistributingUpdateProcessorFactory` processor.

Let's see how we can use this processor in Solr and stop the automatic distribution of documents to shards:

1. We'll update `solrconfig.xml`, which available at `%SOLR_HOME%/example/solr/collection1/conf`, with the following lines:

   ```
   <updateRequestProcessorChain>
     <processor
       class="solr.NoOpDistributingUpdateProcessorFactory"/>
     <processor class="solr.LogUpdateProcessorFactory"/>
     <processor class="solr.RunUpdateProcessorFactory"/>
   </updateRequestProcessorChain>
   ```

2. After making the change, we'll upload the configuration to Zookeeper using this line:

   ```
   $ $SOLR_HOME/example/scripts/cloud-scripts/zkcli.sh -zkhost
   localhost:9983 -cmd upconfig -confdir %SOLR_HOME%/example/solr/
   collection1/conf -confname default
   ```

3. We'll then reload the collection using the following command:

   ```
   $ curl
   "http://localhost:8983/solr/admin/collections?action=RELOAD&name=m
   usicCatalogue-solrcloud&wt=json&indent=2"
   ```

4. After reloading the configuration, we'll post some data to one of the shards and see whether the automatic distribution of documents has been stopped or not.

   Let's send some data to the `Shard 1` (`Port 8983`) instance using the following command:

   ```
   $ curl -X POST -H 'Content-Type: application/json' 'http://
   localhost:8983/solr/musicCatalogue-solrcloud/update' --data-binary
   '
   [
   ```

```
    {
      "id": "3",
      "title": "I should go in Shard 1"
    },
    {
      "id": "4",
      "title": "I should also go in Shard 1"
    }
  ]'
```

After running this query, we'll get the following response if everything goes successfully:

```
{
  "responseHeader": {
    "status": 0,
    "QTime": 0
  }
}
```

Now let's run a query against Shard 1 to check whether the documents that we've indexed go to Shard 1 or not:

```
wget http://localhost:8983/solr/musicCatalogue-solrcloud/select?q=*%3A*&w
t=json&indent=true&distrib=false
```

After running this query, we can see the following output:

```
{
  "responseHeader": {
    "status": 0,
    "QTime": 0,
    "params": {
      "q": "*:*",
      "distrib": "false",
      "indent": "true",
      "wt": "json"
    }
  },
  "response": {
    "numFound": 3,
    "start": 0,
    "docs": [
      {
        "id": "2",
```

```
      "title": [
        "Apache Solr Cookbook"
      ],
      "_version_": 1516224138192093184
    },
    {
      "id": "3",
      "title": [
        "I should go in Shard 1"
      ]
    },
    {
      "id": "4",
      "title": [
        "I should also go in Shard 1"
      ]
    }
  }
 ]
 }
}
```

We've seen from the preceding example how we can easily stop the automatic distribution of indexed documents to other shards in the cluster.

Previously, we saw how we can use the distrib flag in Solr to query individual shards. Solr also provides us with a shards flag, which we can use to query an individual shard or a group of shards for documents. Let's see how we can use this flag in Solr:

- **Single shard**:

  ```
  curl "http://localhost:8983/solr/musicCatalogue-solrcloud/select?q
  =*:*&shards=localhost:8987/solr"
  ```

- **Group of shards**:

  ```
  curl "http://localhost:8983/solr/musicCatalogue/select?q=*:*&shard
  s=localhost:8987/solr,localhost:8983/solr"
  ```

Summary

In this chapter, we saw how we can use SolrCloud to easily create a cluster of Solr servers, which can be used to scale our Solr instances. We also saw how we can easily use the Collections API provided by Solr to manage shards or replicas.

In the next chapter, we'll cover a case study of how Solr is used in e-commerce websites to enhance the user experience while searching for products or a catalogue.

11

Case Study of Using Solr in E-Commerce

In the previous chapter, we saw how we can use SolrCloud to set up a cluster of Solr servers, which can be used to provide a fault-tolerant and high availability environment. Now let's see how we can use Solr in e-commerce websites to improve user experience while searching for a relevant product. Providing the best user experience is the main concern for e-commerce websites these day, and we can use Solr's inbuilt features to provide a much better search experience for the user.

In this chapter, we'll cover the following topics:

- Creating an AutoSuggest feature
- Result grouping and facet search
- Search filtering and sorting
- Relevancy boosting

Creating an AutoSuggest feature

One of the most common features that we can see in today's e-commerce websites is an AutoSuggest feature, which provides users with a list of available content. Let's see how we can create this feature using `Solr`. `Todo` this, we'll use the following steps.

Let's create a new core in Solr and call it `musicStore`. After we have created the core, we'll create a new `schema.xml`. It will contain the following fields:

```
<!-- Unique Id -->
<field name="id" type="string" indexed="true" stored="true"
required="true" multiValued="false"/>
```

```xml
<!-- Song name -->
<field name="songName" type="string" indexed="true" stored="true"
required="true" multiValued="false"/>


<!-- Artist name -->
<field name="artistName" type="string" indexed="true"
stored="true" required="true" multiValued="false"/>
<!-- Album Artist -->
<field name="albumArtist" type="string" indexed="true"
stored="true" required="false" multiValued="false"/>


<!-- Album name -->
<field name="albumName" type="string" indexed="true" stored="true"
required="true" multiValued="false"/>


<!-- Duration of the Song -->
<field name="songDuration" type="double" indexed="true"
stored="true" required="false" multiValued="false"/>


<!-- Duration of the Song -->
<field name="composer" type="string" indexed="true" stored="true"
required="false" multiValued="false"/>


<!-- Song rating -->
<field name="rating" type="float" indexed="true" stored="true"
required="false" multiValued="false"/>


<!-- Year which the song has been published -->
<field name="year" type="int" indexed="true" stored="true"
required="false" multiValued="false"/>


<!-- Genre of the song (e.g. rock, pop, indie, etc)-->
<field name="genre" type="string" indexed="true" stored="true"
required="false" multiValued="false"/>


<!-- Price -->
<field name="price" type="float" indexed="true" stored="true"
required="false" multiValued="false"/>
<!-- Sale -->
<field name="sale" type="boolean" indexed="true" stored="true"
required="false" default="false" multiValued="false"/>


<!--Suggestions field -->
<field name="txtSuggestions" type="suggestType" indexed="true"
stored="true" multiValued="true"/>
```

We'll also create a new `fieldType` in `schema.xml`; it will hold the tokenized values of `songName`. This will use `WhitespaceTokenizerFactory` to create tokens of the indexed value:

```
<!--Suggestion FieldType -->
  <fieldType name="suggestType" class="solr.TextField"
    positionIncrementGap="100">
    <analyzer>
      <charFilter class="solr.PatternReplaceCharFilterFactory"
        pattern="[^a-zA-Z0-9]" replacement=" "/>
      <tokenizer class="solr.WhitespaceTokenizerFactory"/>
      <filter class="solr.StandardFilterFactory"/>
      <filter class="solr.LowerCaseFilterFactory"/>
      <filter class="solr.RemoveDuplicatesTokenFilterFactory"/>
    </analyzer>
  </fieldType>
```

In the `suggestType` field type, we've used filters to tokenize the words that are getting indexed into Solr and make sure that we're not indexing any duplicate data in them. More information about the filters used can be found on the Solr Wiki at `https://wiki.apache.org/solr/AnalyzersTokenizersTokenFilters`.

After making the changes in `schema.xml`, we'll add a `searchComponent` of the `solr.SuggestComponent` type in `solrconfig.xml`. The `searchComponent` will provide us with suggestions depending on the field that we specify. In this case, we're using the `txtSuggestions` field, which will contain the song name that has been tokenized during indexing:

```
<!--SearchComponent -->
  <searchComponent name="suggestComponent"
    class="solr.SuggestComponent">
    <lst name="suggester">
      <str name="name">customSuggester</str>
      <str name="lookupImpl">BlendedInfixLookupFactory</str>
      <str name="suggestAnalyzerFieldType">suggestType</str>
      <str name="blenderType">linear</str>
      <str name="minPrefixChars">1</str>
      <str name="doHighlight">false</str>
      <str name="weightField">score</str>
      <str name="dictionaryImpl">DocumentDictionaryFactory</str>
      <str name="field">txtSuggestions</str>
      <str name="buildOnStartup">true</str>
      <str name="buildOnCommit">true</str>
    </lst>
  </searchComponent>
```

Once we have added the `searchComponent`, we'll add a search handler with the path as `/suggest`, which we can use to suggest the song name:

```
<!--Suggest Request Handler -->
<requestHandler class="solr.SearchHandler" name="/suggest"
  startup="lazy" >
  <lst name="defaults">
    <str name="suggest">true</str>
    <str name="suggest.count">10</str>
    <str name="suggest.dictionary">customSuggester</str>
  </lst>
  <arr name="components">
    <str>suggestComponent</str>
  </arr>
</requestHandler>
```

In this `searchHandler`, we're referencing the `suggestComponent` that we added in the previous step. The following attributes are set in the custom search handler:

- `suggest`: If this is set to `true`, it will use `suggestComponent`.

- `suggest.count`: This is the maximum number of suggestions that the handler should return.

- `suggest.dictionary`: This is the name of the dictionary to use. In our case, it's `customSuggester`, which we've specified in `searchComponent`.

> More information about the attributes can be found at `https://cwiki.apache.org/confluence/display/solr/Suggester`.

After setting up `schema.xml` and `solrconfig.xml`, we can index some data into the core. We can use the `sampleMusicStoreData.csv` included in the `Chapter 11` code ZIP file by executing the following command:

```
curl 'http://localhost:8983/solr/musicStore/update?commit=true' --
data-binary @sampleMusicStoreData.csv -H 'Content-type:application/csv'
```

After indexing the documents, we can navigate to the following URL, which will suggest song names that start with "A":

```
http://localhost:8983/solr/musicStore/suggest?q=A&wt=json
```

We'll get this response from the Solr server:

```json
{
  "responseHeader":{
      "status":?0,
      "QTime":?0
    },
    "suggest":{
      "analyzing":{
        "A":{
            "numFound":?2,
            "suggestions":[
              {
                "term":"<b>A</b>ll I Want For Christmas Is You",
                "weight":?0,
                "payload":""
              },
              {
                "term":"<b>A</b> Thousand Years",
                "weight":?0,
                "payload":""
              }
            ]
        }
      }
    }
}
```

We can see from the response that the component has returned two suggestions that start with "A".

Facet navigation

We've seen previously how Solr provides a facet, by using which we can put indexed data into groups depending on the fields. Let's see how we can improve user experience while selecting the type of music by grouping music into genres.

We can use facet=true to enable faceting of fields, and then use facet.field=genre to return the number of songs that are in each category. The search query will return only the facet data and will look like this:

```
http://localhost:8983/solr/musicStore/select?q=*%3A*&start=0&rows=0&wt=json&indent=true&facet=true&facet.field=genre
```

As we're interested in the facet data only, we've specified `rows=0`. This URL will return us the following data:

```
{
    "responseHeader":{    },
    "response":{    },
    "facet_counts":{
        "facet_queries":{ },
        "facet_fields":{
            "genre":[
                "Pop", 3,
                "Dance/Electronic", 2
            ]
        },
        "facet_dates":{},
        "facet_ranges":{},
        "facet_intervals":{}
    }
}
```

As the user can be presented with the number of songs available under each genre, he/she can then click on the genre to further his/her search for the song that he/she is looking for. In the next section, we'll see how we can use the filters available in the search handler to further refine search results.

Another way in which we can group data is by using the group parameter. Grouping provides us with a way to return the top *N* documents (the default value is 1) by field. Let's see how we can use this feature:

```
http://localhost:8983/solr/musicStore/select?q=*%3A*&wt=json&indent=t
rue&fl=id,songName,genre&group=true&group.field=genre&group.limit=10
```

The URL will return the following response; we have currently used the `fl` parameter, which tells Solr to return a set of fields from the index:

```
{
    "responseHeader":{
        "status":0,
        "QTime":1
    },
    "grouped":{
        "genre":{
            "matches":5,
            "groups":[
                {
                    "groupValue":"Pop",
                    "doclist":{
```

```
            "numFound":3,
            "start":0,
            "docs":[
                {
                    "id":"1001",
                    "songName":"Don't Stop the Party",
                    "genre":"Pop"
                },
                {
                    "id":"1002",
                    "songName":"All I Want For Christmas Is
                        You",
                    "genre":"Pop"
                },
                {
                    "id":"1003",
                    "songName":"A Thousand Years",
                    "genre":"Pop"
                }
            ]
        }
    },
    {
        "groupValue":"Dance/Electronic",
        "doclist":{
            "numFound":2,
            "start":0,
            "docs":[
                {
                    "id":"1004",
                    "songName":"Killing the Light",
                    "genre":"Dance/Electronic"
                },
                {
                    "id":"1005",
                    "songName":"Not Giving In (Radio Edit)",
                    "genre":"Dance/Electronic"
                }
            ]
        }
    }
  ]
 }
}
}
```

From the result, we can see that the group.field parameter has grouped the genre into two categories: Pop and Dance/Electronic. Also, group.limit=10 tells the search handler to return the top 10 results for each category.

Search filtering and sorting

In the previous section, we saw how we can use the facet feature to group data together and seethe number of results in each genre. We can use the `fq` parameter to further limit the search. Let's now see how we can use the `fq` parameter to return only those songs whose genre is `Pop`:

```
http://localhost:8983/solr/musicStore/select?q=*%3A*&wt=json&indent=true&fq=genre:Pop&fl=id,songName,genre
```

This URL will result in the following output:

```
{
    "responseHeader":{
        "status":0,
        "QTime":2
    },
    "response":{
        "numFound":3,
        "start":0,
        "docs":[
            {
                "id":"1001",
                "songName":"Don't Stop the Party",
                "genre":"Pop"
            },
            {
                "id":"1002",
                "songName":"All I Want For Christmas Is You",
                "genre":"Pop"
            },
            {
                "id":"1003",
                "songName":"A Thousand Years",
                "genre":"Pop"
            }
        ]
    }
}
```

As we can see from the preceding output, the results are limited to those songs whose genre is `Pop`. This example shows us how we can apply filters to results.

We can also sort the data using the `sort` parameter, which we can specify. Let's see how we can sort the `songName` in ascending order:

```
http://localhost:8983/solr/musicStore/select?q=*%3A*&wt=json&indent=t
rue&fq=genre:Pop&fl=id,songName,genre&sort=songName%20asc
```

The preceding URL gives the following result:

```
{
    "responseHeader":{
        "status":0,
        "QTime":0
    },
    "response":{
        "numFound":3,
        "start":0,
        "docs":[
            {
                "id":"1003",
                "songName":"A Thousand Years",
                "genre":"Pop"
            },
            {
                "id":"1002",
                "songName":"All I Want For Christmas Is You",
                "genre":"Pop"
            },
            {
                "id":"1001",
                "songName":"Don't Stop the Party",
                "genre":"Pop"
            }
        ]
    }
}
```

Relevancy boosting

Let's see how we can boost some documents in Solr. Relevancy boosting can be very helpful in e-commerce websites to promote some products. In our `musicStore` core, we've specified a `Boolean` field called `sale`, which will tell whether the song is available for sale or not. While showing the results to the user, we can boost the documents that have `sale=true` in them.

We'll need to index the `sampleMusicStoreData2.csvfile` to Solr, as it contains more data about songs, which is needed for this example. We can use the following command to index the file:

```
curl 'http://localhost:8983/solr/musicStore/update?commit=true'
--data-binary @sampleMusicStoreData2.csv -H 'Content-type:application/
csv'
```

We can now use the following URL to see the indexed documents that are available for sale and whose `artistName` matches `Rihanna`:

```
http://localhost:8983/solr/musicStore/select?q={!boost%20b=sale}artis
tName:Rihanna&wt=json&indent=true&fl=id,songName,sale&rows=100
```

```
{
    ▾ responseHeader: {
          status: 0,
          QTime: 1
      },
    ▾ response: {
          numFound: 16,
          start: 0,
        ▾ docs: [
            ▾ {
                  id: "1012",
                  songName: "S&M",
                  sale: true
              },
            ▾ {
                  id: "1013",
                  songName: "What's My Name? (feat Drake)",
                  sale: true
              },
            ▸ { … },
            ▸ { … },
            ▸ { … },
            ▸ { … },
            ▸ { … },
            ▸ { … },
            ▸ { … },
            ▸ { … },
            ▸ { … },
            ▸ { … },
            ▸ { … },
            ▸ { … },
            ▸ { … },
            ▾ {
                  id: "1020",
                  songName: "You Da One",
                  sale: false
              }
          ]
      }
}
```

From the preceding output, we can see that it returns those documents whose sale field is set to true first, and then it returns those documents whose sale field is set to `false`.

 More information about boosting of documents can be found at `https://wiki.apache.org/solr/SolrRelevancyFAQ`.

Summary

In this chapter, we covered the various features of Solr that can be used in an e-commerce website to provide a better user experience while searching results. Solr being open source provides an easy way to plug new features into it.

This chapter covered mostly the common features that are used in e-commerce and how to recreate those features in Solr.

This is the last chapter of the book, and we've now covered the various ways in which we can index data in Solr. This should give us enough skills to use this indexing feature of Solr in some real-life projects (for example, web crawlers, e-commerce websites, extracting data from word documents, and so on). Also, there are lots of books and online resources that will be useful for you all to get a deeper understanding of the features that have been discussed in this book.

Index

A

analyzers
about 13-15
phases 15, 16
running 22, 23
Apache Nutch
about 69
installing 70-72
URL 70
used, for Solr configuration 73-77
Apache Tika
about 63
configuring, in Solr 63-65
atomic updates
using, in Solr 82-85
autoSoftCommit
config elements 81
AutoSuggest feature
creating 121-124

C

collections API, SolrCloud
about 108-111
supported operations 106
URL 111
content streaming 97-99
copy fields 30
cores, Solr
managing 11
URL 12
CSV
URL 48
used, for indexing updates 48

cURL
URL 44
custom search handler
attributes 124
Cygwin
URL 70

D

data, indexing from MySQL
about 51
datasource, configuring 51-55
DIH commands, running 55-57
data, indexing
about 25-27, 39-42
copy field 30
dynamic fields 30
fields, defining 28, 29
field types 27, 28
unique key, defining 30
datasource
configuring 52-55
DIH commands
about 55
delta import 55
for aborting current import 56
for checking status 56
for reloading configuration 55
full import 55
URL 55, 56
directory structure 9, 10
distributed indexing 114-118
documents
about 10
adding 42, 43
deleting 44, 45

P

parser interface 63
PDF
  indexing 65-67
porter stem filter 21
processor factory
  URL 91
products
  searching 114-118

R

RealTime get
  reference link 86
  using 85-87
relevancy boosting
  about 129-131
  URL 130, 131
replication, SolrCloud 112
request handlers
  about 41
  mapping, ways 42

S

search filtering 128
sharding, SolrCloud 112
SignatureUpdateProcessorFactor class
  enabled 95
  fields 94
  overwriteDupes 95
  signatureClass 94
  signatureField 94
single JSON document
  adding 46
soft commit 79-81
Solr
  about 1
  Apache Tika, configuring 63-67
  architecture 8, 9
  atomic updates, using in 82-85
  configuring, with Apache Nutch 73-76
  cores 10-12
  dashboard, URL 5
  data, indexing 25
  data, inserting 39-42
  directory structure 8, 9

group of shards 118
  installing, in Linux 6, 7
  installing, in OS X (Mac) 2
  installing, in Windows 3-5
  overview 1
  query browser, URL 80
  running 2, 3
  single shard 118
  text fields, analyzing 14, 15
  UIMA, integrating with 99-101
  UpdateRequestHandler, configuring 42
  URL 6
Solr Admin UI
  using 32-35
SolrCloud
  collections API 108-111
  configuration files, updating 111, 112
  setting up 103-106
sorting 128
standard tokenizer
  about 17
  example 17
supported operations, collections API 106
synonym filter 20

T

tika-example 63
tokenizers
  about 13-18
  keyword 17
  lowercase 18
  N-gram 18
  standard 17

U

unique key
  defining 30
Unstructured Information Management
    Architecture (UIMA)
  about 99
  integrating, with Solr 99-101
  URL 99
UpdateRequestHandler
  configuring 42
updates
  indexing, with CSV 48

W

Windows
  Solr, installing 3
Word documents
  indexing 65-67

X

XML
  elements 42, 43
  used, for indexing documents 42
XPath
  used, for indexing data 57-61

Thank you for buying
Apache Solr for Indexing Data

About Packt Publishing

Packt, pronounced 'packed', published its first book, *Mastering phpMyAdmin for Effective MySQL Management*, in April 2004, and subsequently continued to specialize in publishing highly focused books on specific technologies and solutions.

Our books and publications share the experiences of your fellow IT professionals in adapting and customizing today's systems, applications, and frameworks. Our solution-based books give you the knowledge and power to customize the software and technologies you're using to get the job done. Packt books are more specific and less general than the IT books you have seen in the past. Our unique business model allows us to bring you more focused information, giving you more of what you need to know, and less of what you don't.

Packt is a modern yet unique publishing company that focuses on producing quality, cutting-edge books for communities of developers, administrators, and newbies alike. For more information, please visit our website at www.packtpub.com.

About Packt Open Source

In 2010, Packt launched two new brands, Packt Open Source and Packt Enterprise, in order to continue its focus on specialization. This book is part of the Packt Open Source brand, home to books published on software built around open source licenses, and offering information to anybody from advanced developers to budding web designers. The Open Source brand also runs Packt's Open Source Royalty Scheme, by which Packt gives a royalty to each open source project about whose software a book is sold.

Writing for Packt

We welcome all inquiries from people who are interested in authoring. Book proposals should be sent to author@packtpub.com. If your book idea is still at an early stage and you would like to discuss it first before writing a formal book proposal, then please contact us; one of our commissioning editors will get in touch with you.

We're not just looking for published authors; if you have strong technical skills but no writing experience, our experienced editors can help you develop a writing career, or simply get some additional reward for your expertise.

Apache Solr Enterprise
Search Server

Third Edition

ISBN: 978-1-78216-136-3   Paperback: 432 pages

Enhance your searches with faceted navigation, result highlighting, relevancy-ranked sorting, and much more with this comprehensive guide to Apache Solr 4

1.   An update to the popular second edition of Apache Solr 3 Enterprise Search Server, covering Solr 4's most important new features such as SolrCloud for scaling and real-time search.

2.   Contains integration examples with databases, web crawlers, Hadoop, XSLT, Java and embedded Solr, PHP and Drupal, JavaScript, and Ruby frameworks.

Apache Solr High Performance

ISBN: 978-1-78216-482-1   Paperback: 124 pages

Boost the performance of Solr instances and troubleshoot real-time problems

1.   Achieve high scores by boosting query time and index time, implementing boost queries and functions using the Dismax query parser and formulae.

2.   Set up and use SolrCloud for distributed indexing and searching, and implement distributed search using Shards.

3.   Use GeoSpatial search, handling homophones, and ignoring listed words from being indexed and searched.

Please check **www.PacktPub.com** for information on our titles

Apache Solr 4 Cookbook

ISBN: 978-1-78216-132-5   Paperback: 328 pages

Over 100 recipes to make Apache Solr faster, more reliable, and return better results

1. Learn how to make Apache Solr search faster, more complete, and comprehensively scalable.

2. Solve performance, setup, configuration, analysis, and query problems in no time.

3. Get to grips with, and master, the new exciting features of Apache Solr 4.

Apache Solr Beginner's Guide

ISBN: 978-1-78216-252-0   Paperback: 324 pages

Configure your own search engine experience with real-world data with this practical guide to Apache Solr

1. Learn to use Solr in real-world contexts, even if you are not a programmer, using simple configuration examples.

2. Define simple configurations for searching data in several ways in your specific context, from suggestions to advanced faceted navigation.

3. Teaches you in an easy-to-follow style, full of examples, illustrations, and tips to suit the demands of beginners.

Please check **www.PacktPub.com** for information on our titles